Cross Purposes

"This book describes a manner of following Jesus that is 'more counter cultural than most Americans can imagine.'"
—Ray Bakke

Cross Purposes

Exploring the Crossroads of Justice and Reconciliation

Mark Miller

Foreword by Ray Bakke

WinePressPublishing
Your Book, Defined. Since 1991.

© 2010 by Mark Miller. All rights reserved.

WinePress Publishing (PO Box 428, Enumclaw, WA 98022) functions only as book publisher. As such, the ultimate design, content, editorial accuracy, and views expressed or implied in this work are those of the author.

No part of this publication may be reproduced, stored in a retrieval system, or transmitted in any way by any means—electronic, mechanical, photocopy, recording, or otherwise—without the prior permission of the copyright holder, except as provided by USA copyright law.

Unless otherwise noted, all Scriptures are taken from the *Holy Bible, New International Version®, NIV®*. Copyright © 1973, 1978, 1984 by Biblica, Inc.™ Used by permission of Zondervan. All rights reserved worldwide. WWW.ZONDERVAN.COM

ISBN 13: 978-1-4141-1769-0
ISBN 10: 1-4141-1769-8
Library of Congress Catalog Card Number: 2010903745

To Bethlyn, my wife...my bride,
who for over thirty years has demonstrated
unconditional love.

More than any other human being, you have
shown me what it means to love and to be loved.

Contents

Foreword ix

Introduction xv

  1. Rudiments 1
  2. Reorientation 31
  3. Redemption 55
  4. Recapitulation 77
  5. Resolution 99
  6. Relevance 127

Scriptures Cited 141

Works Cited 145

Bibliography 151

Endnotes 161

Foreword

MARK MILLER HAS blown my cover in this book. Since spending a few weeks with Orthodox scholars in 1976, and with a host of near eastern Protestant scholars like Dr Kenneth Bailey, over subsequent years in my role as a founder and current chair of Evangelicals for Middle Eastern Understanding, I've quietly come to understand and modify my western theological heritage at a few profound points, including mission theology and the true significance of Christ's work on the cross.

In mission, I remember well the Armenian bishop who reminded me that in the west we usually think of the great commission in horizontal terms—the going to the far corners of the globe, and in this generation, because it is now possible, at least for us. By contrast, he suggested, he thinks of the Great Commission as a vertical commitment of faithful witness of Christians who steward faith in this one place for 2,000 years, often while forbidden to travel. Of course, it can be both, but it was so wonderfully helpful to see Christian mission history as multi-dimensional.

Cross Purposes...

As a pastor and husband and father of three sons, while living amid the crucible of inner city Chicago for thirty-five years, I watched the vengeance and wrath of people and powerful social systems up close and personal. Meanwhile, in the Middle East, and increasingly in the west, I am sickened by news of so-called "honor killings," where fathers or brothers kill and torture sons and daughters to somehow restore honor to a family. How such murders truly restore honor mystifies most of us, I suspect.

It seems an increasing number of contemporaries ask that same question about our God, who seems unable or unwilling to forgive us without an honor killing to preserve an eternal honor code. But that is how many interpret God's execution of his Son on the cross and how preachers and poets explained it in schools, sermons, and songs, especially in our western tradition, both before and after the Reformation, where grace and reconciliation was defined for so many of us.

Thirty-four years ago, my eldest son, Woody, brought home his friend Brian from school. Then for about six months, we fed him, most often by gigantic lunches made by Corean and carried to school each day for Brian. Brian had been homeless off and on all his life, but when he got sick, we decided to move him into our house. But for medical treatment, we needed a legal status. I found his birth mom, who told me I could have him. I voluntarily, and almost for free (he cost me $80.00 in a court fee), adopted Brian and declared him my son. A month later, and late one Sunday night, he told us that he had decided to become a Christian. He said, "I see how it works, Dad. You sent your son into my world and into my school. He became my friend, and because you love your son, when he brought me into this family, you adopted me. I see now that God sent Jesus into

Foreword

the world, and anybody who becomes a friend of Jesus gets loved and adopted by God into the family."

Brian had nailed it. In Bible School, college, and seminaries, I'd studied Bible, theology, and missions, and I was then teaching church history and pastoring, but I never heard it more plainly put. God did not send Jesus into the world to kill him on the cross for us. Jesus voluntarily left heaven and went to what he knew was a God-awful death on a Roman cross to rescue, reclaim, and reconcile us, the way Ken Bailey had so wonderfully described it with his Middle Eastern understanding of the Prodigal Son story of Luke 15.

What Mark Miller does in this manuscript is he provides a truly "fresh look" and such practical ways to talk about the unconditional love of God, modeled in a marriage to Bethlyn, lasting as long as Jesus lived among us to show us that same unconditional love of the Father. Mark uses stories by C. S. Lewis and others to reinforce his practical teaching, while explaining the Greek New Testament sparingly and simply.

That all this emerged from a men's Bible class with his paraglider pilots, when one of them asked, "Why would anyone want to be adopted by a God who treated his own kid that way?" speaks to a major dilemma of our time, and that is people's faulty view of God.

Corean and I saw a terrifying example of what I call this "faulty folk faith" back in 1970, when we used our first two-week vacation to visit Appalachia to study the sending culture of people I was trying to pastor in Chicago. We met a missionary pastor named Arnold Johnson, who had lived and served in east Tennessee among poor mountain people for thirty-three years. His children had married and still lived there in what was clearly their adopted home.

Then Arnold's wife got cancer, died, and was buried in that community, after which the congregation shunned the pastor and stopped coming to church. Just when he needed compassion, they mystifyingly, but cruelly, recoiled and asked, "Why is God punishing the pastor? He must have committed awful sins." Their view of cancer as punishment for sin nearly destroyed him. He finally left. Arnold ended up in Chicago, and we saw him a few times over the years.

God is not vengeful, a lesson Staupitz was trying to get the young Luther to understand. Luther had understood God was angry and vengeful, permitting the devil freedom to torture him in this life, and that God would continue it forever in eternity. The love of Christ finally won him over. The gospel is good news, not good advice. It is what Jesus did and not what we do. We can be forgiven and restored because Christ's rightness is put like a robe over our sin and filth, and we "switch kingdoms" as followers.

Well into the book, I finally realized why I think Mark invited me to comment on his work. He's been coming with me the past few years into the Orthodox world of Middle Eastern churches, and he clearly shows the theological perspective of some long-time friends and colleagues. Contemporary scholars such as Tom Oden and the late Robert Webber, who taught for years where I taught seminary in Chicago, call this "ancient future" theology. Whatever you choose to call us, I will insist that we are *not* liberal, but clearly radical. The Orthodox had fewer lawyers defining influencing centuries of their theological tradition. They nuance and parse the salvation story in less legal ways. Following Jesus the way Mark has learned from the earliest church fathers and modern story tellers like C.S. Lewis will make following Jesus more counter-cultural than most Americans can imagine.

Foreword

You help us all. I'm out of the closet, Mark, and finally in print on this, thanks to you.

To God be the glory.
    And to the earth be peace.
To the paragliders be thanks.
    And to our world be hope!

—Ray Bakke
Chancellor and Professor
Bakke Graduate University
Seattle, Washington

Introduction

For God so loved the world that He gave His one and only Son, that whoever believes in Him shall not perish but have eternal life.

—John 3:16

"YOU SAY THAT since I am a Christian, God has adopted me as a son. Well, I'm not so sure I want to be his child, considering how he treats his kids!"

I confess the comment caught me a bit off-guard. "What do you mean?" I asked, struggling for time to formulate an answer. "Why in the world wouldn't you want to be adopted as God's child?"

"Well, you say that God couldn't just sweep my sins under the carpet—that someone had to pay for my sin. Then you tell me God loves me so much that he couldn't bear to see me pay for it, so he punished Jesus instead. I guess I'm not sure I want to be God's child if he would punish another one of his kids for something he didn't even do. What kind of a Father is he, anyway?"

"What kind of a father is he, anyway?" For the past several years, I have been on a quest to answer that question—specifically, I have been on a quest to better understand exactly what God did when he took on human flesh, lived among us, and died in our place. It was a quest that began innocently enough on a Tuesday night at a Bible study I was leading. Little did I know how profound that moment in time it would prove to be, for before we were done, the seeds were sown for a spiritual journey that would literally change my life. This book is the product of my quest.

First, let me share with you a bit of background. My name is Mark Miller, and I pastor a small church in a small Washington town called Issaquah, which is nestled in the foothills of the Cascade Mountains just east of Seattle. If you leave Seattle and head east for about thirty minutes on Interstate 90, you'll quickly (and I do mean quickly!) pass through Issaquah. Yes, to the casual traveler Issaquah is just a bump in the road—a final place to gas up before traversing Snoqualmie Pass through the Cascade Mountains, leaving the moist temperate climate of the Puget Sound and entering the more extreme, arid, environs of eastern Washington. Boasting just over 11,000 official inhabitants, according to the 2000 census (around 50,000 within a five-mile radius), this former coal mining/now young professional bedroom community sits, at least for the moment, on the eastern border of Seattle's ever-expanding suburban sprawl. It is a suburban community that still has the hometown feel of its earlier, more rural days.

My family and I have lived and ministered in Issaquah for over twenty years—it is our home. In addition to my normal pastoral duties, I also lead a weekly Bible study for a group of paraglider pilots. Though a small town, Issaquah is home to a world-class paragliding center.[1] Year-round,

Introduction

hundreds of pilots—some local, others from all over the world—launch off the summit of nearby Tiger Mountain and invade the skies over Issaquah to enjoy the mild conditions and incomparable scenery of the beautiful Pacific Northwest. It is truly a spectacular place to fly.

I started flying almost ten years ago as a diversion from the stress and strain of daily vocational ministry. My wife was not surprised, for paragliding had a natural attraction for me. Years ago, before I was married, I taught skydiving. However, once I met the girl I would marry, skydiving gradually faded from the picture. But the passion for flying remained. Years later, when we moved to Issaquah, I discovered a skydiving center right in the middle of town. To my chagrin, the center closed soon after we moved in. Still, every so often, something resembling a parachute appeared in the air near Tiger Mountain. I later learned that a new sport called "paragliding" had taken root in our community. Within a very short time I, too, was hooked!

Paragliding seemed like a natural evolution of my original skydiving passion. And from my wife's practical point of view, it was far cheaper than skydiving (no fuel!). Also, from all appearances, it seemed inherently safer (but she still cringes when she hears an ambulance siren screaming south of town).

I quickly discovered that paragliding gave back to me something life had stolen. All of my troubles seemed to slip away as I spiraled heavenward, free from the confines of office, society, and cell phones. I found myself soaring serenely with the bald eagles and red-tailed hawks that make Tiger Mountain their home.

The Christian pilots among us jokingly refer to paragliding as "rapture practice," referring to that future moment described in 1 Thessalonians in which all the Christ-followers, both dead and alive, are "caught up together…

in the clouds to meet the Lord in the air" upon His glorious return (1 Thessalonians 4:17). We figure this event, which theologians call "the rapture," will be much like paragliding...just without the glider! It definitely gives us a special sense of anticipation as we await Jesus' return.

As a pilot who is also a pastor, God has opened the door for me to minister to many of my fellow flyers. Over the years, I have become sort of a flying field chaplain, helping distressed pilots sort through troubled marriages, lost jobs, various addictions, and even the occasional injury or death. One such avenue of ministry is my weekly Bible study for pilots. While I did not start this particular gathering (it was initiated by another pilot, who is now a missionary in Chile), I have led these Bible studies for most of the past decade. God has used them to truly change lives. I have a photograph in my office of one of the pilots, dripping wet and grinning from ear to ear, as he emerged from the chilly waters after a lake baptism. Through my flying ministry, I have come to realize that the best evangelism occurs when you simply "do life" with those around you.

This Bible study has truly been a blessing to me as well. However, it has also been something of an eye-opening experience, for most of the flyers in my Bible study are not exactly your typical church folks. Paraglider pilots, like most adrenalin junkies, tend to be somewhat nontraditional, eclectic, and even a bit rough around the edges. This reality was driven home to me one evening when I asked the group to open their Bibles to a particular passage we were going to study. One of the "newbies" in the group turned to me, raised his hand, and in complete innocence, asked (with some frustration), "Where the hell is Romans, anyway?"

Over the years, I have come to realize how much this group reflects the kind of people Jesus hung around—honest, hardworking folks who call life like they see it. These

Introduction

are people who don't necessarily have the most flowery speech, people who, like James and John, could be called "sons of thunder." What I have found so interesting is how much I prefer to be around them as well. I've also learned that there is tremendous benefit to "doing life" with folks who are not quite like me...or at least not like the person I'd like to think I am! That's probably a good thing, because the people in my church are also very diverse!

Someone in town referred to our particular congregation as "The Church of Last Resort." Far from being critical, they were merely observing that people who felt out of place in other churches often feel right at home in ours. I think that is because our regulars have learned to look beyond the exterior and see the face of Jesus in those who might not quite fit the profile of the average church attendee. I am truly blessed!

That brings me back to the night—that night when my quest began. We were gathered, as usual, in the paragliding school classroom. We had finished our obligatory warm-up time, playing ping-pong and watching "blooper" film of the previous week's flying mishaps (the school instructor is never without his video camera). We had settled into our circle of chairs, prayed for one another, and opened our Bibles. So far, everything was normal.

I do not recall the particular passage we were studying, but I remember we were discussing the love God has for each and every one of us. I was sharing about God's invitation to be adopted as his sons and daughters—to literally become part of His family. And then, the statement: "Well, I'm not so sure I want to be his child, considering how he treats his kids!" And then, the question: "What kind of a father is he, anyway?"

I recovered quickly (remember, I'm a pro!). In typical pastoral fashion, I cobbled up an answer that seemed to satisfy him. The problem was, my answer failed to satisfy me. I had always struggled with the notion that Jesus was punished, that he was a victim rather than a victor. My flying friend's question only reminded me of an existing perplexity that had lain dormant until he disturbed it. And once he asked the question—once he gave this conundrum life through words—I could no longer shove it back into the recesses of denial. It was out in the open, and I could not ignore it. And so my quest began.

The result of this quest was a journey that led me back to school, around the world, and into a new level of freedom in Christ that I have never known before. It is my prayer that you will continue reading and, in so doing, experience some of this same freedom for yourself. For I have come to believe the real work of God in Christ is even more amazing and even more hopeful than I ever realized before. I pray this becomes your realization as well.

Your fellow pilgrim,
Mark Miller
Issaquah, Washington
2010

Chapter 1

Rudiments

Amazing love! How can it be that Thou, my God, shouldst die for me?
"And Can It Be That I Should Gain"
—Charles Wesley, 1738

IN HIS SECOND mystical tale of spiritual warfare, Christian fiction writer Frank Peretti paints a vivid scene. A monumental battle had taken place between the army of heaven and the rebels of evil, culminating in a victory for the forces of the King, with parallel manifestations of victory in the physical realm. Unseen by human eyes, the heavenly host have decisively routed the forces of darkness, while on earth, the precious souls of yet a few more lost lambs enter the fold of the Shepherd. Several of the victorious angelic warriors look upon this tender scene of new birth in Christ. "Redemption," one of them remarks wistfully. "It will never cease to thrill me."[2]

I know exactly what he meant, for as many times as I have read the old, old story, as many times as I have seen it played out in the lives of men and women who have turned from darkness to light, from death to life, I still don't understand it. I can only stand amazed. It is with this amazement and failure to completely grasp its enormity that I endeavor to examine the atoning work of Jesus Christ—a topic that has befuddled and continues to stretch and confuse the greatest theological intellects in history. Knowing this, there is a part of me that wonders what business I have jousting with issues that have unsettled far better minds than mine. However, mine is a practical quest, undertaken with some degree of urgency, for I need real solutions for real people dealing with real issues. I need answers for folks who are asking questions upon which their very eternity is hanging. At the very least, I need to better understand this amazing event wherein God "emptied himself of all but love and bled for Adam's helpless race."[3] If I cannot understand it, I must at least raise my confusion to a higher level!

This opening chapter is simply entitled "Rudiments." According to the dictionary, a rudiment is a basic principle or element. It is a foundational component of something greater in size or importance. Things that are rudimentary are basic in nature—elemental. Rudiments are baseline concepts upon which greater complexity is assembled. Given that we are looking to "build" a new understanding of what exactly Jesus accomplished for us and why, it seems it would be wise to first consider the basic elements—the rudiments—before "getting creative."

All human creativity, at best, mimics God's creative work. As creatures made in his image, we have inherited the creative DNA from our parent. When we exercise our latent creativity, we are simply joining a process that is already underway. In fact, it has been ongoing since the dawn of eternity.

Rudiments

To the Jews, God's role as Creator is one of his most important attributes. Only God truly creates. When the apostle John introduces God as having taken on human flesh in the opening lines of his gospel account, he immediately portrays Jesus in the role of Creator: "In the beginning was the Word, and the Word was with God, and the Word was God. He was with God in the beginning. Through him all things were made; without him nothing was made that has been made" (John 1:1–3).

The Jews understood the difference between God's creative work and human creativity, and they used different Hebrew words to describe these processes. Since God fashioned everything from nothing—in Latin, *ex nihilo*—the Hebrew word *bara* is used to describe God's creative activity. On the other hand, human creativity is defined as *asah*, which refers to the fact that, at best, we can rearrange material already present.[4]

This distinction between genuine creativity and mere rearrangement is especially appropriate in this particular discussion, for as the writer of Ecclesiastes reminds us, "there is nothing new under the sun" (Ecclesiastes 1:9). Simply put, all any of us can really do is rearrange the material already in front of us. Entitling this chapter "Rudiments" seemed appropriate, for it seeks to assemble the existing material with which we shall work and explores how others have "created" with it in the past. The chapters that follow then propose a different "arrangement."

The Foundation

The first step in any building construction project is to lay a foundation upon which the rest of the structure may be safely and securely constructed. A similar foundation is needed for our discussion of Jesus' atoning work on our behalf. Fortunately, much of that foundation is already firmly in place. It is also worth noting that much of the existing edifice resting on that foundation is structurally sound. In a sense, our project is not so much new construction as it is remodeling. It is an undertaking intended to improve upon what already exists, not to replace it. So before we can begin work on the new addition, we need to carefully examine the older, existing structure to determine what stays and what goes.

Recently, I had to repair the chimney on our home. Water stains and puckering paint on the ceiling told me something was amiss, and it all seemed to be oriented around the chimney. So, one warm spring day, I went up on the roof to see if I could figure out what was needed. To my dismay, I discovered crumbling brick and missing mortar had virtually eliminated any water-tight integrity the chimney had once possessed. I called in a mason, who started dismantling the old chimney from the top down. He removed anything faulty or even suspect until he finally reached a foundation of strong, sound brick and mortar. Then, he rebuilt the chimney back to its original dimensions, complete with new flashing and chimney caps. Once the chimney was sealed, my water problems were a thing of the past.

In a similar fashion, our project requires an examination of the subject before us. We must determine which elements of our current understanding are solid and worth keeping and which should be jettisoned in favor of new material. In the end, the overall shape of our subject may look similar to what appeared before we started. We are still left with the fact that Jesus took on human flesh; lived a perfect life; died on a cross for our sins; and rose again from the dead as a testimony to his power (and ours) over sin, death, hell, understood that he would not undertake any roof repair work. I appreciated these details and his specifying the intended work, for it kept me from developing unrealistic expectations.

Every project requires scoping; every undertaking needs parameters. The beginning parameter for our project is the definition of our subject. Our project is best defined as a re-examination of what is typically known in Christian circles as "the atonement." I suspect this is not a totally unfamiliar term. Anyone who has spent much time in church has heard at least a passing reference to the atonement. What I find surprising is that many people, when pressed, find themselves at a loss to explain what this particular word really means. For our purposes, any reference to the term "atonement," will mean the work Jesus accomplished when he took on human flesh, lived a perfect life, suffered a violent death on the cross, rose gloriously from the grave, and empowered us with his resident Spirit. If this definition of "atonement" seems a bit different—perhaps a bit broader than expected—I would ask your indulgence. In the course of our study together, I shall try to explain why I define "atonement" as broadly as I do.

Since I was working with an existing term, my initial research focused on understanding the root of the word "atonement." Through the magic of Google, I searched the internet for helpful references. After slogging past various films and rock bands bearing that title, I finally came across a Catholic Encyclopedia entry that offered the following:

> The word *atonement*, which is almost the only theological term of English origin, has a curious history. The verb "atone," from the adverbial phrase "at one" (M.E. *at oon*), at first meant to reconcile, or make "at one," from this it came to denote the action by which such reconciliation was effected.[5]

Scholar and theologian C. I. Scofield connects this relatively modern English term with the Hebrew word "kaphar," though he cautions that it is not an actual verbatim translation:

> The English word "atonement" (at-one-ment) is not a translation of the Hebrew kaphar, but a translator's interpretation. According to Scripture the legal sacrifice "covered" the offerer's sin and secured the divine forgiveness; according to the translators it made God and the sinner at-one. But the O.T. sacrifices did not at-one the sinner and God. "It is not possible that the blood of bulls and goats should take away sins" (Heb 10:4). The Israelite's offering implied confession of sin and of its due dessert, death; and God "covered" (passed over, Rom. 3:25) his sin, in anticipation of Christ's sacrifice, which did, finally, "put away" the sins "done aforetime in the forbearance of God."[6]
>
> —Ro 3:25; Heb 9:15

Catholic scholar Richard John Neuhaus observes, "'Atonement.' It is a fine, solid, twelfth-century Middle English word, the kind of word one is inclined to trust. Think of at-one-ment: What was separated is now at one."[7]

reconciliation.

A check of *The Holman Bible Dictionary*[9], *Elwell's Dictionary of Theology*[10], *The Expository Dictionary of Bible Words*[11], *Noah Webster's 1828 Dictionary*,[12] and even the current *Merriam-Webster Dictionary*[13] revealed pretty much the same thing in terms of defining "atonement." Bottom line—atonement—"at-one-ment"—is really, first and foremost, a process whereby two or more parties (usually) who were separated are reconciled—are made one.

However, this is certainly not a unanimous view. Other scholars, while acknowledging a reconciliatory outcome of atonement, focus more comprehensively on the notion of satisfying God's wrath. In his enduring *Systematic Theology*, Louis Berkhof notes that the "moving cause of the atonement" lies in the "good pleasure of God" who was "so good and loving that the very idea that sinners would be hopelessly lost was abhorrent to Him. Therefore He offered Himself as a victim in their stead, paid the penalty by laying down His life for transgressors, and thus pacified an angry God."[14] And while Berkhof does not specifically address the notion of "at-one-ment," he does indicate that the reconciliation represented by this term must be "understood as something that is secondary. The reconciled God justifies the sinner who accepts the reconciliation, and so operates in his heart by the Holy Spirit, that the sinner also lays aside his wicked alienation from God, and thus enters into the fruits of the perfect atonement of Christ. In other words, word "atonement" transcends typical theological camp boundaries. Louis Berkhof is stridently Calvinist. However, Wesleyan scholar J. Kenneth Grider also takes issue with the notion of "at-one-ment" as a definition, stating, "A popular notion is that 'atonement' means 'at-one-ment.' This is incorrect because 'atonement' refers only to the provision for 'at-one-ment.'"[16] For Grider, the mechanism of atonement is distinct from its manifestation.

For the purposes of our discussion regarding the incarnation, life, death, and resurrection of Jesus, let us say, then, that the atonement means, specifically, God's effort in Christ to draw wayward humanity back into a saving and abundant relationship with him. We were separated from God by our sin—by our rebellion, our betrayal. And God took the initiative whereby we were, again, made one with him.

This is what the apostle Paul had in mind when he wrote, "…that God was reconciling the world to himself in Christ, not counting men's sins against them" (2 Corinthians 5:19). Note that it is God in Christ doing the reconciling. We do not reconcile ourselves to God; he reconciles the world to himself. No matter which atonement theory one examines, virtually all of them agree it was God who took the atoning initiative. Our role is merely one of response.

The root impetus of God's atoning work is a desire on his part for reconciliation with his fallen human creation. It is this reconciling aspect of atonement that led me, as previously noted, to group not only Jesus' death on the cross (the more narrow and common understanding) but also his birth, life, resurrection, and spiritual indwelling under this heading. For all these aspects of Jesus' existence perform a role in the more overarching work on God's part to draw us back into intimacy—to reconcile us to himself. All are part of God's eternal effort in restoring us to the intimacy with him—the "at-one-ment"—we were created to enjoy.

Although we have our definition, the question is whether or not this definition is clear enough. We must admit that, pardon the expression, the devil is in the details! The mechanics of reconciliation—of atonement—are anything but clear. Through the ages, countless faithful scholars have sought to explain this most mysterious work of God. As I have researched this topic, I have come to appreciate just how important their quest for precision truly was, for one's view of the atonement literally shapes one's view of the very character of God himself. And one's view of God's character inevitably shapes his or her response to him.

Throughout Scripture, God reveals himself, among other ways, as a father—in fact, as a loving, heavenly Father. And yet, even so simple a metaphor can be fraught with baggage. Personally, I have no difficulty with this analogy, for I had an earthly father who loved me and was kind to me. However, through the years, as I have sought to portray God in fatherly terms to others, I have frequently encountered great emotion on the part of those for whom the image of "father" was decidedly negative. This often painful view of their own earthly father became a cloudy lens through which they viewed everything their heavenly Father did. Consequently, if their earthly father's actions were suspect, God's work in their lives quickly fell under suspicion as well. What I have often discovered is that a lot of time, care, and patience on the part of loving friends and family is often required before these individuals are able to cultivate any other more positive response. Clearly, how we perceive God's character affects our understanding of everything God does, and of why he does it.

This, then, became the issue behind my Bible study friend's question. For in his mind, what God "did" to Jesus on the cross was incongruent with the image of God as a loving Father. How could a Father who truly loves his children ever inflict them with such pain and suffering? He understandably questioned why anyone would ever enter into such a potentially damaging relationship of their own volition. My friend is not alone in his confusion.

I have discovered that most people's perception of God lands somewhere in the spectrum between two unhealthy extremes. On the one hand is the view that God is first and foremost a vindictive judge who must punish each and every offense committed against him. Consequently, God is perceived as a cranky old man with a stick who is just looking for someone on whom he can pound. The other extreme reflects a diametrically opposed understanding of God as a pushover grandfatherly type who cannot bear to see anyone suffering or unhappy. This portrayal is essentially a heavenly version of television's Mr. Rogers who, complete with sweater and sneakers, just wants to be our neighbor. Neither extreme accurately captures God's holy character or his heart for humanity.

It quickly becomes apparent that our discussion is more than just esoteric theorizing best left to the rarified atmosphere of a library or seminary. This is no heady debate akin to an argument over how many angels can fit on the head of a pin. Rather, this is an intensely practical and personal pursuit that affects every single one of us. As I said, one's understanding of the atonement literally shapes one's view of the very character of God. And that view, in turn, dictates that person's response to all God has done for us in Christ.

The Existing Structure

As previously mentioned, the discussion of Jesus' atoning work on the cross is not a new one. Ever since Jesus was born, lived, died, rose from the dead, and ascended to heaven, the world has been struggling to understand exactly what happened at that wonderful, awful moment when heaven and earth met and God offered up his life for his beloved human creation. As one might expect, abundant theories have been proposed over the years in an attempt to explain an event that quickly proves to be somewhat unexplainable. In order to orient ourselves in this discussion, a short review of the current understanding, together with the path the church has followed in getting there, is appropriate.

The following is a brief working summary of the three most prevalent atonement theories or models. There were certainly others, but the rest tended to be more variations or combinations of these three primary theories than new theories in and of themselves. As we consider each of them, we must remember that they were inevitably shaped by the cultures that spawned them. The same is true of any new conclusions we may draw. For we, like all those theological sleuths before us, are peering at the evidence through the lenses of our culture. And it is quite difficult to remove them. Instead, we are better served by merely admitting these lenses exist and by seeking to compensate for them whenever possible and practical. And we need not fear this cultural "adulteration," for part of the miracle of the atonement is its ability to transcend these inevitable human influences.

The Christus Victor Model

The first explanations of why Jesus had to die were formulated by the early church fathers, those pioneering theologians and churchmen who primarily lived and worked during the first three centuries after his death and resurrection. This was a time of tremendous political intrigue and religious fervor, particularly in Rome and the empire to the east. Religious convictions during this time could make one unpopular or, even worse, could make one dead! Given the oppressive nature of the society in which they lived, and their perpetual hope for deliverance, it is not surprising these early scholars saw in the atonement the elements of a cosmic conflict between God and the forces of evil. And it is significant to note that these explanations served the church almost universally for the first thousand years—the first half of its existence.

In a series of lectures delivered at the University of Uppsala (Sweden) in March and April of 1930, Lutheran pastor and scholar Dr. Gustaf Aulén labeled this conflict-centered view of Jesus' work as the *Christus Victor* or classical model of the atonement. He used this term to contrast and refute what he labeled the Latin view (the satisfaction doctrine that had its beginning in the original Roman Church and developed during the Reformation—see below). There were two main "flavors" or versions of *Christus Victor* thinking embraced by the early church.[17] It is to these we now turn our attention.

Recapitulation

One of the earliest *Christus Victor* views was set forth by Irenaeus of Lyons, an early church father who lived during the middle to late second century (A.D. 130–200). One of

Irenaeus's chief contributions to the atonement discussion was his proposition that God viewed sin not so much as a crime to be punished, but rather as an impediment to the relationship he longed to have with his precious human creation. Revealing what today would be considered a more Eastern Orthodox view of sin (i.e., as a disease to be healed rather than a crime to be punished), Irenaeus saw the cross of Christ not as an instrument of punishment, but as a symbol of victory wherein Satan is defeated and the way is made clear for humanity to live in new freedom with their Creator. Irenaeus observed:

> Man had been created by God that he might have life. If now, having lost life, and having been harmed by the serpent, he were not to return to life, but were to be wholly abandoned to death, then God would have been defeated, and the malice of the serpent would have overcome God's will. But since God is both invincible and magnanimous, He showed His magnanimity in correcting man, and in proving all men, as we have said; but through the Second Man He bound the strong one, and spoiled his goods, and annihilated death, bringing life to man who had become subject to death. For Adam had become the devil's possession, and the devil held him under his power, by having wrongfully practiced deceit upon him, and by the offer of immortality made him subject to death. For by promising that they should be as gods, which did not lie in his power, he worked death in them. Wherefore he who had taken man captive was himself taken captive by God, and man who had been taken captive was set free from the bondage of condemnation.[18]

More specifically, Irenaeus saw the victory Jesus won on the cross in terms of what he called "recapitulation" (from a

Greek word ανακεφαλαιωσις [A-na-KEF-a-lī-Ō-sis]—"to bring to a head"). He wrote, "God recapitulated in himself the ancient formation of man and woman, that He might kill sin, deprive death of its power and vivify humanity."[19] I find it interesting to note that this is the same Greek word Paul employs in his letter to the Romans, wherein he says all God's commandments are "summed up" or recapitulated in one rule: "Love your neighbor as yourself" (Romans 13:9).

This notion of recapitulation is, perhaps, best illustrated in the Old Testament observance of *Yom Kippur*—the Day of Atonement (see Leviticus 16). On this holiest day of the Jewish calendar, the high priest, with great ceremony, sacrificed a bull as a sin offering for himself. Then he selected two goats without spot or blemish for use in atoning for the sin of Israel. The first goat was slaughtered, and its blood was sprinkled upon the atonement cover in the Holy of Holies and upon the Tent of Meeting, thereby purifying the people and reconciling them to God. Next, after cleansing the altar, the high priest laid his hands on the head of the second goat and, on behalf of the entire nation, ceremonially transferred onto it the sin of the people. The hapless goat was then sent away into the wilderness. One assumes it was quickly killed by predators.

In other words, the sin of the people was transferred onto the spotless purity of the goat and taken away, while, at the same time, the spotless purity of the goat was imparted to the sinful people. (For a dramatic and illustrative allegory of this idea of recapitulation, read *The Ragman* by Walter Wangerin, Jr.[20]) Perhaps it was this recapitulation imagery that lay behind the exclamation of John the Baptist when he beheld Jesus: "Look, the Lamb of God, who takes away the sins of the world!" (John 1:29). (It is worth noting that in the Old Testament, the term "animal from the flock" is often translated "lamb" and refers to the offspring of both sheep and goats, which were often kept in a mixed flock and were both used for sacrificial purposes.[21])

Ransom

Another variant of *Christus Victor* thinking springs from the very words of Christ himself. In Mark's gospel, we read that Jesus said, "The Son of Man did not come to be served, but to serve, and to give his life as a ransom for many" (Mark 10:45). Most of us, upon reading these words, immediately conjure up a picture of someone paying a sum of money to redeem a kidnapped victim or to recover hijacked property. However, in a first century Palestinian sense, ransom meant something far different. The Greek word translated "ransom" is $\lambda \upsilon \tau \rho o \nu$ (LOO-tron), which refers to the price one paid to secure the legal release of a bondservant from his master.

Frequently, in the ancient world, a person facing financial hardship might indenture himself as a bondservant or slave. Under such a relationship, the indentured individual received room, board, and protection, but no wage. Their wage was their livelihood. Release from this bond service was either through fulfillment of the agreement of indenture or by paying the owner a ransom—a $\lambda \upsilon \tau \rho o \nu$. It is from *this* definition of ransom that the early church understood atonement.

The early church saw the work of Christ as one of ransom and release. This notion developed in an environment wherein many early theologians believed our sin gave Satan certain rights over us. One early church father who held to this school of thought was Athanasius of Alexandria (circa A.D. 293–373), who described the enslaving effect of sin thusly: "Through the transgression sin has subjected the race of men to death's power, and on this account death has legal rights over men."[22] It was as if in betraying God through sin, we left his camp and went over to the enemy, who then became our master.

The ransom view of the atonement is rooted in the belief that Satan, having secured a form of ownership over us as a result of our sin, set the price for our release. And because God loved us and did not wish to see us perish, he paid the asking price—namely, the life of his Son. One of the earliest proponents of this notion of ransom was our friend Irenaeus, who declared, "[Christ] by his blood, gave himself as the ransom for those who had been carried into captivity."[23]

Then, in an incredible display of hubris, Satan inflicted the penalty of sin upon one who had not sinned. Therein was his undoing, for when that happened, Satan not only lost his human slaves, he also lost the ransom payment. Suddenly, in one fell swoop, the evil one was reduced from wealthy slaveholder to impoverished provocateur—he can entice, but he can no longer command. Death, once his means of maintaining control over his charges, was stripped of its power. Like a robber trying to stick up a bank with a rubber gun, Satan was revealed as the usurper he has been from the beginning. "Where, O death, is your victory? Where, O death, is your sting?" (1 Corinthians 15:55).

St. John Chrysostom (347–407), one of early Christendom's most eloquent expositors, reflected on the disarming outcome of Satan's arrogant misstep:

> It is as if Christ said, "Now shall a trial be held, and a judgment be pronounced. How and in what manner? He (the devil) smote the first man, because he found him guilty of sin; for it was through sin that death entered in. But he did not find any sin in Me; wherefore then did he fall on Me and give Me up to the power of death? ...How

is the world now judged in Me?" It is as if it were said to the devil at a seat of judgment: "Thou didst smite them all, because thou didst find them guilty of sin; wherefore then didst thou smite Christ? Is it not evident that thou didst this wrongfully? Therefore the whole world shall become righteous through Him."[24]

However, in spite of the support of such luminaries as Athanasius and John Chrysostom, the ransom view fell somewhat into of a state of disrepute, in part because some of the renditions of it became a bit extreme. Gregory of Nyssa (circa A.D. 335–394), for example, suggested that on the cross, God resorted to a bit of trickery, much like the ploy of a fisherman who disguises the fatal barb of a fishhook with enticing bait. "The Deity was hidden under the veil of our nature, that so, as with ravenous fish, the hook of the Deity might be gulped down along with the bait of flesh"[25] Gregory saw nothing inappropriate in God acting thusly because, as he observed, the devil had first resorted to such tactics, "spreading the glamour of beauty over the hook of vice like a bait."[26] Apparently, Gregory thought the ends justified the means, especially given that Satan did it first!

However, many other theologians were unable to reconcile the purity of God with the notion that he would resort to deception in order to carry out his redemptive plan. Some continued to struggle with the more general suggestion that Satan has any rights over humanity at all, arguing that this concession diminishes God's sovereignty.

However, even though some of the more extreme forms of ransom theology were (rightly) rejected, there remained a fairly general opinion that our sin gave Satan some degree of sway over us—that it gave him certain "rights" that God, in his justice, would not simply ignore. Instead, God offered the asking price for our release—the life of his only Son. It is safe to say that most of the early atonement views (which dominated the first thousand years of the church) embraced some degree of ransom understanding.

Satisfaction

One of the most influential atonement theories came out of the medieval era. Known as the Satisfaction Theory, it had its genesis in the fertile mind of Anselm of Canterbury (A.D. 1033–1109), who most theological scholars readily identify as the champion of reason-based faith. Anselm's seminal work, *Cur Deus Homo* (Why God Became Man), is a thoughtful and comprehensive reflection on both the incarnation and the atonement. Throughout his writing, the influence of the feudal environment in which Anselm lived and worked is reflected.

During the middle ages, European society was very much a culture of "haves" and "have-nots." The "haves" were the aristocracy of the period—the feudal lords who amassed power through the wealth and property they acquired both through inheritance and by conquest. In this era of weak centralized government, the feudal lords were the real power brokers. They ruled their respective empires with an iron hand; their word was law and their power was absolute.

Because they frequently oversaw vast real estate holdings, the feudal lords required considerable manpower to manage their realms. The answer to this personnel problem was found in serfdom. Serfs—the "have-nots"—were indentured or enslaved peasants (often bondservants) who worked the lands of a feudal lord in exchange for sustenance and protection. Serfs had no property of their own and no legal rights beyond what their lord extended to them. Serfs who managed to get on the good side of their feudal masters might enjoy significant favor if their lord was beneficent. However, if the serf was perceived as having somehow insulted his master's honor, satisfaction was the most common requirement. Satisfaction could take the form of monetary or in-kind payment, loss of privilege, or in the case of extreme insult, loss of life. Virtually nothing was beyond the power of the feudal lord to demand and to receive as satisfaction.

> Both honor and satisfaction were of extreme significance in the medieval world of chivalry and feudalism, of knights, lords, and vassals. It was a society of a carefully managed series of reciprocal obligations. The lord provided capital and protection; the serf provided honor, loyalty, and tribute. Honor demanded that a lord do what was proper and act as a lord should act. For example, it would not be proper for a lord to fail to fulfill his pledge of protection of a vassal. Those under the lord must fulfill their oaths of loyalty. If a vassal did not fulfill the requirements of an oath, he must offer something to satisfy the offended lord. It was seen as unbefitting if a lord did not demand redress from a guilty vassal or did not take revenge against another lord who had in some way offended him.[27]

This, then, was the world in which Anselm lived, thought, and wrote. And the influence of his culture emerges constantly throughout the pages of *Cur Deus Homo*. His writing portrays God as a heavenly version of a feudal lord whose honor has been besmirched by his human minions and who, therefore, requires satisfaction. In their discussion of Anselm, writers Joel Green and Mark Baker summarize the effect of this cultural influence upon his writing:

Humans had substituted sinful lives for their vocations of faithfulness and service. Working within a culture characterized fundamentally by the needs of honor and shame (and not, as in much of Western culture, by the concerns of guilt and innocence), Anselm saw that the human predicament was the consequence of the human assault on God's honor.[28]

Anselm's work represents a departure from earlier ransom thinking in that it focuses less on the efforts of the devil and concentrates more on the offenses humanity committed against God. In book two, chapter seven of *Cur Deus Homo*, Anselm wrote:

> I believe, moreover, that those who think the devil has some right in justice to hold man in possession, come to this conclusion because they see that it is just for man to be subjected to abuse by the devil, and that it is just for God to permit this, and consequently they think it is just for the devil to inflict it.[29]

Since humanity committed the wrong, humanity must make it right. Jesus, as our representative, made satisfaction for the stain on God's honor through his substitutionary death on the cross. Simply put, Jesus paid the penalty to God that we should have paid.

However, it is important to note that Anselm's view of satisfaction was not rooted in punishment, but in sacrifice. Jesus, God incarnate, died in our place, not as a recipient of divine punishment but as the only pure and spotless human sacrifice that could adequately atone for humanity's transgression. "'Satisfaction' for us, in our criminal-justice system, has to do with the apprehension and punishment of the guilty, while for Anselm and his contemporaries, satisfaction hinged on the fulfillment of certain obligations related to loyalty and honor."[30] The transition from sacrifice to punishment, which is now part and parcel of Western atonement thinking, would be introduced, largely, by our next theological luminary, Thomas Aquinas.

Thomas Aquinas (A.D. 1225–1274) was one of the more scholarly men of his age. Steeped in the traditions of the Dominicans, Thomas sought to find a balance between faith and the reasoning that was increasingly invading his world. As a result of that quest, Thomas wrote voluminously. His *magnum opus* was the enormous *Summa Theologica*, which is considered one of the finest examples of theological systemization the world has ever seen. It is safe to say that in Thomas, scholasticism reached its high water mark. Regardless of what one might think of his views, it is impossible to deny the symmetry of his systematic thinking. Even his detractors are forced to acknowledge that Saint Thomas, as he came to be known, is one of the greatest theologians of all time. With regard to the atonement, he rejected the ransom theory in favor of Anselm's satisfaction view:

> The payment of satisfaction is treated as the essential element in Atonement and as accomplished by the death of Christ; the payment is primarily the work of Christ's human nature, but it gains increased meritorious value on account of the union of human nature with the Divine nature in Christ. So Thomas Aquinas teaches explicitly: the human nature of Christ makes the offering, but, because He is God, the merit of His work is not merely sufficient, but superabundant.[31]

However, unlike Anselm, who saw Jesus' death as sacrifice, Thomas speaks of Jesus as enduring punishment, which is the more common understanding of satisfaction thinking. The notion of penance also developed out of this same stream of thought. Not surprisingly, the atonement view of Thomas Aquinas (as well as his theology in general) has been largely adopted by the current Roman Catholic Church.

In keeping with the trend of their cultures, both Anselm and Thomas Aquinas pursued a logical, rational path in explaining the atoning work of Christ. However, the notion of satisfaction did not really become systemized until it fell into the hands of the greatest systematic theologian of the Reformation era, John Calvin (A.D. 1509–1564). An attorney by trade, Calvin's detailed mind and legal framework was ideally suited to the work of systematizing Reformation theology. He went about it with great zeal, constantly expanding the reservoir of his burgeoning thoughts until what began as a 516-page book swelled to become a multi-volume opus that consumed over 1,700 pages.

Perhaps more than any other Reformation theologian, Calvin addressed the notion of the atonement. Embracing Anselm's view of satisfaction, Calvin concluded that the offense of sin was not so much an assault on God's honor as it was a violation of his justice. Perhaps the impetus for this shift in thinking rests in the juridical nature of Calvin's prior profession. Calvin wrote, "God in his character of Judge is hostile to us, expiation must necessarily intervene, that as a priest employed to appease the wrath of God, he may reinstate us in his favour."[32]

Calvin's understanding of atonement as rooted in justice formed the foundation for the later work of Charles Hodge, the American reformed theologian of the nineteenth century who, more than anyone else in modern times, defined the penal substitution model of the atonement that is so deeply entrenched in current Western theological thought. It is to Hodge's work that we now briefly turn our attention.

Charles Hodge (A.D. 1797–1878) is important primarily because of his impact upon modern Western thinking with regard to the atonement. A prolific writer, Princeton-educated Hodge was the author of an enormous three-volume systematic theology that, initially published in 1872, continued to roll off the presses as late as 1981. More than any other modern theologian, Charles Hodge developed what has become known as the Penal Substitution Theory of the atonement. It would be safe to say that this particular view is the one most commonly taught in modern Western churches and is, at least subliminally, embraced by most modern Western Christians.

Hodge declared God cannot simply pardon sin "without a satisfaction to justice, and he cannot have fellowship with the unholy."[33] Further, he argues that God's justice "demands the punishment of sin. If sin be pardoned, it can be pardoned in consistency with divine justice only on the ground of a forensic penal satisfaction."[34] In fact, Hodge suggests that one of the hallmarks of God's moral excellence is his punishment of sin.[35] In light of such thinking, it is easy to see how the notion of the atonement as a punitive event became so rooted in Western Christendom.

The Moral Influence Model

The third significant atonement theory or model also came out of the medieval era and was advanced by scholar Peter Abelard (A.D. 1079–1142). Abelard was one of the more tragic figures in Christian history. Forcibly castrated by the misinformed and anguished father of his young and pregnant mistress, Abelard endured a difficult existence, even by medieval standards. However, in spite of his considerable life challenges, he was also a brilliant intellect as well as a prolific writer.

Like Anselm, Abelard also questioned the purpose behind the incarnation. And, like Anselm, Abelard rejected the idea that Jesus was the currency of a ransom payment to Satan. However, he disagreed with Anselm's notion that Jesus was the satisfaction rendered to a dishonored deity. Instead, Abelard concluded that Jesus was an example—a model of the life God wants all his followers to embrace and a graphic portrayal of the gravity of sin, which put perfect love to death. Jesus serves as an inspiration to all who are seeking spiritual wholeness and a deterrent to all who would follow the appetites of the flesh. "'Our redemption is that greatest love kindled in us by Christ's passion,' for 'kindled by so great a benefit of divine grace, love should not be afraid to endure anything for his sake.'"[36]

Simply put, the death of Jesus was not efficacious in and of itself—it did not render satisfaction as Anselm suggested or constitute a ransom payment as Irenaeus proposed. Instead, the death of Jesus served as an inspiration to godly living and a caution against the evil of sin. By observing the depth of God's love and the lengths he was willing to go on our behalf, we in turn are motivated by that love to also take up our crosses and follow him.

Abelard's view never cultivated the substantial following enjoyed by the *Christus Victor* or Satisfaction theories. Notable among those who did build on Abelard's foundation was the seventeenth century Unitarian philosopher Faustus Socinius, who denied the pre-existence of Jesus. Thoroughly antitrinitarian, Socinus believed salvation came by following the path of devotion that Jesus blazed for us.[37] Nineteenth century German theologian Frederick Schleiermacher also pursued an exemplary theme in his theology,[38] as did twentieth century English utilitarian philosopher Hastings Rashdall.[39] Most modern atonement views acknowledge

Jesus' value as an exemplar; however, they repudiate the suggestion that the value and influence of His incarnation, life, death, and resurrection is solely influential.

In conclusion, the Penal Substitution Theory has become the *de facto* explanation of the atonement. Sin has become a crime, and punishment is the requirement. It is neat, and it is systematic. And yet, as the reaction of my friend in Bible study illustrates, the Penal Substitution view of the atonement still leaves something to be desired.

Still, if one is going to take issue with a particular principle, one had best be able to offer a satisfactory alternative. It is to this task we shall now turn. However, there is one small consideration we must first address.

Attitude Check

Before I take off in my paraglider, I always do a pre-flight check. I do this to ensure that there are no preexisting conditions that may adversely affect my flight. One of my instructor's "blooper" videos features a flyer who forgot to fasten the leg straps on his harness before taking off. As he begins his takeoff run, the glider lifts skyward, and he slips out of the harness, tumbling down the hillside as his glider, now pilotless, flies off into the sunset. Fortunately, he was not injured (not all such incidents end so positively); and his glider landed, undamaged, in a field some time later, where it was easily retrieved.

In aviation, an equipment check is essential before taking off. In an endeavor such as ours, an attitude check is similarly essential. "Pre-flighting" our particular endeavor—in this case, launching a new understanding of the atonement—doesn't involve too many equipment details other than, perhaps, securing a steaming cup of coffee and a comfortable reading chair. However, we do need to conduct an attitude check to make sure we are mentally, emotionally, and spiritually ready for the task at hand.

So far, we have tried to examine the atonement through the eyes of those who have come before us; for it is their perceptions that provide the necessary foundation for future discussion. As we consider each of their views, it is important for us to remember the passion that prompted their formulation. In our modern era, we are gifted with a plethora of resources upon which to draw in studying Scripture and developing doctrine. Whether written, audio, video, online, or live, we in the new millennium have unprecedented access to information and opinion. We are, arguably, the most well-informed generation in the history of humanity. Oh, that we were equally obedient to what we know!

Most of our current base of data was collected and processed by those who have come before us. We stand tall only because we stand upon their shoulders. We can avoid needlessly bleeding where others have already bled. Truly, we are indebted to those early thinkers whose ideas we now examine in minute detail. Thanks to the 20/20 lens of hindsight, we can microscopically dissect the views of some of these early believers. Unfortunately, we often employ that historically enhanced scrutiny with a marked lack of sensitivity and grace.

I have always enjoyed church history—I love reading the stories of the early pioneers of the Christian faith. Truly, they are superheroes! Unfortunately, this is often not the way their lives and ministries are portrayed. All too often in reading historical accounts of the work of these early trailblazers, I am distressed to note how frequently those whose views we currently deem marginal are labeled as heretics by modern writers. It seems there is a certain "my way or the highway" attitude that, all too often, pervades current Christian thinking. It is this uncharitable, myopic view that frequently provides fertile soil wherein the enemy sows his inevitable seeds of discord.

Speaking politically, someone once observed that the only difference between a freedom fighter and a terrorist is whether or not they won their struggle. In other words, those on the winning side of a conflict are hailed as freedom fighters, regardless of the tactics they used to secure victory. Those on the losing side are condemned as terrorists, even though their tactics may not have been any more egregious than those of the victors.

This same attitude often seems to lie behind the labeling of orthodoxy and heresy. Certainly there is a place—an important one—for doctrine and dogma, and I salute those who labor to help us construct accurate doctrinal frameworks. However, as the apostle Paul enjoined, we must, over everything, "put on love" (Colossians 3:14). Simply put, we are called to maintain a certain balance in our pursuit of proper doctrine. We must always be discerning, but never in a condescending or self-exalting way.

I would go so far as to suggest that we are as indebted to those we may view as being in error as we are to those whose positions we readily embrace. For all of these pioneers have contributed greatly to our current understanding. As I seek to develop a more practical working view of the atonement, I do so with a tremendous sense of awe and respect for those whose views now serve as grist for my relatively pedestrian mill. I have great appreciation for the enormous contribution their work makes toward any improvement in understanding my efforts may facilitate. The fact that I may not agree with some of their conclusions does not mean I value their contribution to my understanding any less.

One final note: The chapters that follow describe the different aspects of the work of atonement God performed for us in Christ. By necessity, one chapter follows after another, and the reader might take this to mean they describe some sort of a "sequence of salvation" on God's part—that one element of the atonement is a precursor to the others. However, the Bible hints that God may not be constrained by the time-space continuum as we are. The apostle Peter reminds us that "with the Lord a day is like a thousand years, and a thousand years are like a day" (2 Peter 3:8). The apostle John indicates that God's redemptive activity took place outside the human confines of space and time. In the Revelation, he describes this transcendent mystery when he declares that Jesus, the sacrificial Lamb of God, was "slain from the creation of the world" (Revelation 13:8).

For the purpose of illustration, think of a time when you watched a parade. Now, let's extend that imagery to encompass the myriad of events in one's life. We time-constrained humans must observe the parade of life from the curbside of our physical, chronological human existence. We see the beginning of the parade, then the middle, and finally, the end, all sequenced in time. However, from God's ten-thousand-foot view, the entire parade of eternity is visible, simultaneously, from beginning to end. There is no sequence—no time-sensitive component. That's because God lives in what theologian Paul Tillich called the "eternal now," wherein every aspect of eternity is a present reality.[40] If you are like me, you can quickly develop a headache trying to wrap your brain around such notions. However, we must understand that our salvation is both a recognized reality and an ongoing operation. For we have been saved (the new birth—Ephesians 2:8–9), we are being saved (sanctification—2 Corinthians 4:16), and we shall be saved (glorification—1 Peter 1:5). Truly, the work God has done, is doing, and shall do transcends even time.

In like fashion, each of the operations described in the following chapters is both simultaneous and interwoven. God the Father, God the Son, and God the Holy Spirit were acting, are acting, and shall act in unison to bring about the salvation of the human race. It is my limitation as a writer and yours as a reader that necessitates our examining both the operations and the operators one at a time.

REFLECTION QUESTIONS

1. Prior to beginning our journey together, what was your understanding of the atoning work of Christ?

2. What does "atonement" mean? How does the notion of atonement apply to you?

3. What are the three main theories of the atonement that have shaped modern thought? Can you briefly summarize each of them? Their strengths? Their weaknesses?

4. Explain the idea of ransom as it pertains to the atonement. What are the pros and cons of this theory?

5. Explain the idea of recapitulation as it pertains to the atonement.

6. What is the main weakness of the moral influence theory?

Chapter 2

Reorientation

What language shall I borrow to thank Thee, dearest friend, For this Thy dying sorrow, Thy pity without end? O make me Thine forever, and should I fainting be, Lord, let me never, never outlive my love to Thee.
"O Sacred Head Now Wounded"
—Bernard of Clairvaux, 1153

IT IS A fact that one's understanding of the goal defines the tactics used in getting there. In our earlier discussion, we saw how, over time and through culture, the church, particularly in the West, came to view God's pursuit of justice as the overriding concern in interpreting the atonement. Everything God did, therefore, in executing the atonement was analyzed through that culturally induced, juridical lens. However, it is a natural corollary to such thinking that a faulty understanding of the goal leads to a faulty assessment of the pursuant tactics. I would suggest that this is precisely what has happened in the development of our current understanding of the atonement. We have gotten off-center with respect to God's overarching purpose in his atoning work, and we need a reorientation around a proper center if we have any hope of acquiring a better understanding of why God acted as he did.

Our earlier examination of the origins of the word "atonement" yielded relational roots wherein it is equated with reconciliation. One can make a strong case that the gospel itself, rooted in immanence as it undeniably is, is equally relational in nature. Consequently, I want to suggest that relationship—specifically, the reconciliation of relationship, not justice, is God's overriding concern in the atonement process. I believe that the etymology of the word "reconciliation" supports this claim.

The most common New Testament word for "reconcile" is καταλλασσω (kah-tah-LAH-sō). Paul is the only New Testament writer who uses this word to describe the unique reconciliation between God and humanity. Used in this sense, καταλλασσω:

> ...denotes a transformation of the state between God and us and therewith of our own state, for by it we become new creatures (2 Cor. 5:18), no longer ungodly or sinners, but justified, with God's love shed abroad in our hearts (Rom. 5:6ff.). God has not changed; the change is in our relation to him and consequently in our whole lives.[41]

According to the dictionary, the root of the English word "reconcile" can be traced to the Latin prefix "*re*," which simply means "to do again," and the root word "*conciliare*," which means "to assemble, to unite, to win over."[42] So, the overarching purpose of God's atoning work in Christ is the "uniting again" of a holy God and his wayward human creation. Notice the absence of any hint of punitive or judicial flavor. For truly, "God did not send his Son into the world to condemn the world, but to save the world through him" (John 3:17).

The Bible is clear that it was our sin—our betrayal or our rebellion—that separated us from God in the first place. Because of this sin, the intimate fellowship for which we were created was frustrated. As Paul noted, "What fellowship can light have with darkness?" (2 Corinthians 6:14). However, because of the atoning birth, life, death, and resurrection of Jesus, the sin-gulf between God and humanity was spanned, and the intimacy for which we were created was restored. Concerning this monumental work, the apostle Paul rejoiced:

> But now in Christ Jesus you who once were far away have been brought near through the blood of Christ. For he himself is our peace, who has made the two one and has destroyed the barrier, the dividing wall of hostility, by abolishing in his flesh the law with its commandments and regulations. His purpose was to create in himself one new man out of the two, thus making peace, and in this one body to reconcile both of them to God through the cross, by which he put to death their hostility.
> —Ephesians 2:13–16

The "at-one-ment" language in Paul's declaration is unmistakable.

When justice becomes the focal point, then the punishment of sin takes center stage. However, when relationship becomes the focal point, reconciliation is the overriding concern. Sin does not become unimportant in such a revised framework, but it is positioned in its proper context—as the chief impediment to the relationship with us that God desires and with which he is primarily concerned.

A moment ago, we suggested that our current understanding of the atonement has been improperly shaped by a decidedly judicial and punitive focus. Let's examine a couple of other concepts, the understanding of which has also been skewed by this overly judicial emphasis.

Forgiveness

I want to suggest that the atonement is rooted, first and foremost, in the forgiveness of God, and that forgiveness, like all relational activity, begins in the heart. The Bible teaches that what we do outwardly begins inside. Jesus said, "The good man brings good things out of the good stored up in his heart, and the evil man brings evil things out of the evil stored up in his heart. For out of the overflow of his heart his mouth speaks" (Luke 6:45). In other words, what we do begins in the heart, which in Jesus' day, meant that it sprang from who the person truly was. Consequently, the heart is inevitably the starting point for any relational change.

When a relationship is fractured by offense or injury, someone must take the initiative to repair the breach. For example, at one time or another we all have experienced injury in a relationship. If those relationships experienced healing, it began when someone set aside his or her own pain and took the initiative to restore the connection. Initiative in healing a relationship, inevitably, begins with a desire for reconciliation.

In the case of the wounded relationship between God and humanity, the initiator of reconnection is clearly God—forgiveness begins in his "heart"—in who he truly is. For in our fallenness, we did not, and do not, have the capacity, let alone the inclination, to initiate such a response. "But God demonstrates his own love for us in this: *While we were still sinners*, Christ died for us" (Romans 5:8, emphasis mine). While we were still shaking our rebellious fists in God's face, while we most certainly still did not love him, God *decided* to love us. Clearly, if the relationship was going to be reconciled, God had to take the first step, for we were still living in rebellion and betrayal. As previously noted, in our fallenness, we don't have the ability or even the inclination to heal the relationship. Apart from God's wooing and pursuing, even the desire for reconciliation escapes us. Thankfully, God has equipped us to respond: "For it is by grace you have been saved, through faith—and this not from yourselves, it is the gift of God" (Ephesians 2:8). God gives us the gift of faith, and through exercising that wondrous gift, we are able to respond to God's appeal to reconciliation.

The first step in God's reconciling effort was forgiveness, and it was birthed in the very heart of God. At first blush, forgiveness may seem to be a pretty straightforward concept. However, I have discovered that there actually is a fairly broad spectrum of understanding (or misunderstanding) when it comes to God's forgiveness of sinful humanity. For the next few moments, I want to examine that spectrum.

Frequently, in the Western church, forgiveness is depicted as being transactional—it is something Jesus purchased for us from God by dying on the cross. For example, the beloved old hymn "My Jesus, I Love Thee" intones that Jesus "purchased my pardon on Calvary's tree,"[43] while another popular modern praise chorus declares that Jesus was forsaken so that I could be forgiven.[44] I find this transactional interpretation of forgiveness puzzling given that the mere suggestion of compensation violates the very spirit of forgiveness. Simply put, forgiveness is not forgiveness if it must be purchased or compensated in some way. I haven't really forgiven someone if I was paid to refrain from retaliation.

As an illustration, let us say my neighbor becomes irritated with me and proceeds to throw a rock through my living room window (until recently, when a particularly irascible neighbor finally moved off our street, such an event was not totally unlikely!). Further, let us say my neighbor's companion sees what happens and, fearing my reprisal against his friend, quickly pays me for any needed repairs. As a result, I do not call the police nor do I take my neighbor to court. In summary, I do not exact deserved retribution from my neighbor in any way. I have not retaliated against my neighbor—but have I forgiven him?

While it is true that I do not exact from my neighbor what his offense might warrant, my restraint is not due to any softening of heart on my part. Quite the contrary—my attitude towards my neighbor has probably not changed at all. Inside, I'm still as mad at him as I was before I was paid. I took no action against him simply because I was compensated for not doing so. There is nothing forgiving in my action (or lack thereof). Forgiveness would imply that, though I had the right to compensation, I decided not to pursue such recompense. It is this volitional releasing of the right to compensation that literally defines forgiveness. Simply put, forgiveness (like love) is a decision, not a feeling. It is something I choose to do, freely, as an act of my will.

When Moses renewed the covenant with Israel, he told them that life and death before God was a choice, and he urged them to choose life (Deuteronomy 30:19). James told his readers that life was given to those who love God (James 1:12). Clearly, choosing life is tantamount to loving God, and forgiveness operates in a similar fashion. Moses prayed, "In accordance with your great love, forgive the sin of these people" (Numbers 14:19). Clearly, from God's viewpoint, the decision to forgive is inextricably linked to the decision to love, and loving others will also propel me to forgive.

A compensatory view of forgiveness also fails to explain how Jesus was able to forgive so many people of their sins while he was still alive (for example, the paralytic of Mark, chapter two). How could Jesus say that the man's sins were forgiven if the price for that forgiveness had not yet been paid? Surely, he didn't really say, "Here, take this IOU for your forgiveness. Give me a few weeks, and I'll make it good!"

As we mentioned before, forgiveness is a relational activity. Often, the decision to forgive is rooted in the perceived value of the relationship that has been injured. In the hypothetical case of my broken window, forgiveness implies a decision that the relationship I have (or may have in the future) with my irritated neighbor is worth more than my shattered glass. This decision to pursue relationship rather than recompense is the hallmark of the kind of forgiveness Jesus demonstrated on the cross—it is an act of the will whereby one refrains from seeking the compensation to which they are entitled. It is rooted in the desire to express love…God's love…to those who offend.

We see this unconditional aspect of forgiveness illustrated in Jesus' teaching in Matthew's gospel. In chapter eighteen, Jesus instructed that when we are sinned against, we are to forgive the offender "seventy times seven times" (Matthew 18:22)—in other words, infinitely. There is to be no limit or condition placed upon my forgiveness. Jesus most certainly did not suggest that I should only forgive if I am compensated. And it is a bit morally twisted to suggest that while I am to forgive unconditionally, God needs payment before he is able to forgive. Ephesians 4:32 instructs me to forgive as I am forgiven. Clearly, God's forgiveness of me is the standard to be reflected in my own forgiveness of others.

Recently, I stumbled across an essay by Fr. John Mabry, pastor of Grace North Episcopal Church in California, who, I subsequently learned, is considered to be somewhat of a renegade cleric hovering on the outer fringes of orthodoxy. Because of his questionable doctrine, I was, initially, tempted to discard his essay. However, upon reading further, I discovered that, at least in terms of his understanding of God's forgiveness, he hits the nail squarely on the head. Fr. Mabry asks:

> How can a God who in Jesus told us that we were never to exact vengeance, that we were to forgive each other perpetually without retribution, demand of us behavior that God 'himself' is unwilling or unable to perform?... Why can God not simply forgive as we are instructed to do, rather than mandating that some 'innocent and spotless victim' bear the brunt of 'his' reservoir of wrath? The ability of humans to do this when God will not or cannot logically casts humanity as God's moral superior. This is of course absurd![45]

It is also specious to suggest such forgiveness is rooted in human nature. Surely, if I am to forgive unconditionally, it is only because such forgiveness already has its origins in the heart of God.

The apostle Paul reinforces this notion that our forgiveness of one another is to be patterned after the forgiveness we have already received in Christ: "Bear with each other and forgive whatever grievances you may have against one another. *Forgive as the Lord forgave you*" (Colossians 3:13, emphasis mine). When Jesus said that we are to forgive one another seventy times seven times, he was merely defining a level of expected human forgiveness that was already the gold standard of heaven.

Truly, there has been much misunderstanding in the area of God's forgiveness. I believe much of the disconnection on this subject is rooted in a fundamental misunderstanding of the very nature of forgiveness. And this misunderstanding seems to result from a failure to comprehend the dualistic essence of forgiveness. We often think of forgiveness only from the standpoint of the one offended, without realizing that forgiveness (again, like love) is inherently relational. Both parties in the relationship—and in the dispute—have a role to play and are affected by the outcome. The Greek word most commonly translated as "forgive" in the New Testament is αφιημι, (a-FĒ-ih-mē), which, from a definition point of view, conveys the idea of "release." This is the sense of forgiveness the apostle John uses in declaring that when we confess our sins, God is "faithful and just and will [*release us from*] our sins and purify us from all unrighteousness" (1 John 1:9, emphasis mine).

This understanding of forgiveness as release illustrates its dualistic character—it consists of two components—extension and appropriation. Unlike the Western church, which seems to have a one-dimensional understanding of forgiveness, the Eastern Orthodox Church considers the extension of God's forgiveness to be universal, while the appropriation of it, which provides release and cleansing to the offender, is individual. By way of explanation, Orthodox priest Anthony Coniaris suggests, "...we were all saved [on Calvary], but God will not force this salvation upon us. We must—each of us—accept it personally as the great gift of God's love."[46]

We see this two-dimensional aspect of forgiveness practically worked out in everyday human relationships. For example, I may extend forgiveness to someone immediately for an offense he has committed against me. In so doing, I prevent bitterness from taking root in my heart. Because my forgiveness of the offense (my extension of it) releases me from its grip, I may actually forget about the offense (and even the offender) completely as I go on with my life, which is now unimpeded by what was done to me. Simply put, my extension of forgiveness has set me free.

But what about the offender? Let us say that the offender, on the other hand, refuses to acknowledge his offense or to request my forgiveness for the wrong he has perpetrated against me. So long as he maintains this stiff-necked attitude, he remains in bondage to what he has done, even though the particular offense itself may not reside in his conscious memory. Nevertheless, his offense (unless it is quite minor) will continue to eat away at him, often subliminally, but occasionally popping into his conscious mind when he least expects it (perhaps through a serendipitous encounter with me, the offended party). Finally, perhaps years later, his stubborn heart is finally stricken by what he did; he comes to me, broken, confesses his offense, and receives the release resulting from the forgiveness that was his all along. In so doing, the cycle of extension and appropriation is finally complete, and forgiveness has truly taken place.

Unfortunately, it is not just my relationship with my neighbor that is affected by an unforgiving heart. My relationship with God is also affected. In Matthew's gospel, Jesus taught his disciples, "For if you forgive men when they sin against you, your heavenly Father will also forgive you. But if you do not forgive men their sins, your Father will not forgive your sins" (Matthew 6:14–15). For years, I struggled with this passage because it seemed to suggest God's forgiveness was conditionally rooted in my own behavior rather than springing purely from his grace. However, when I came to better understand the nature of God's forgiveness, this passage became quite clear. Forgiveness flows through forgiveness. In other words, when I have an unforgiving heart, a root of bitterness quickly takes root. When bitterness takes root, it becomes very difficult, if not impossible, for me to experience God's forgiveness and grace. Remember, the root meaning of forgiveness is release. As long as I am withholding forgiveness from my brother, I cannot experience God's forgiving release. Someone once told me, "Harboring bitterness is like taking poison and waiting for the other person to die." An unforgiving heart doesn't do much damage to the unforgiven party, but it does enormous damage to the one withholding forgiveness, not the least of which is its causing that person to have an inability to experience God's release from his or her own sins.

Earlier, I referenced the Eastern Orthodox Church and its therapeutic understanding of forgiveness. Orthodoxy is relevant to our discussion because it represents the oldest existing Christian tradition. From the standpoint of culture and of chronology, the Orthodox Church is closest to the Christian traditions of the early church. Indeed, there are Eastern churches still functioning today that trace their roots back to the first century!

The Orthodox view of sin as a disease to be healed rather than as a crime to be punished informs their understanding of forgiveness. From the Orthodox point of view, the Son did not die so that the Father could forgive; the Father forgave, and the Son died as an expression of that forgiveness and to free us from the sin that prevents us from responding to it.

A friend and colleague of mine, Fr. Mihai Pavel, is a Romanian Orthodox priest. Based near the ancient (they celebrated their 800th anniversary in 2008!) Moldavian and Romanian capital of Iași (pronounced "yosh"), Mihai works for World Vision of Romania, overseeing the many international relationships in which they are involved. During the fall of 2008, I had the privilege of visiting Mihai in his beautiful country and learning more about his particular Christian tradition.

During one of our many conversations, I asked him about the Orthodox understanding of forgiveness. Speaking rather succinctly, he summed up this concept, wherein the incarnation and the cross are the expressions of forgiveness, not the means. Very firmly, he declared, "*Because* God has forgiven, Jesus died."[47] Then, he went on to explain that embracing Jesus is the means by which we appropriate—personally and individually—what God has already extended to us eternally and universally.

Another Orthodox cleric, Fr. Vladimir Berzonsky, further describes this universal extension of forgiveness: "When Scripture says that Jesus Christ, the Son of God, took on human nature in the incarnation, it means that all human beings are given the possibility to receive the very uncreated energy of God by opening themselves to union with the Holy Trinity through incorporation into the God-Man, Christ."[48]

We see this notion in Scripture as well. Earlier we saw how, in his second letter to Corinth, the apostle Paul declared, "…that God was reconciling the world to himself in Christ, not counting men's sins against them" (2 Corinthians 5:19). In other words, Jesus came to earth and took on human flesh as an expression of God's decision *not* to count men's sins against them. Jesus came as a *result* of God's forgiveness, not as a *means* of God's forgiveness. As Fr. Pavel went on to conclude, "God did not have to be satisfied. There was no price on his forgiveness."[49] It was something he freely and lovingly decided to do.

Perhaps this more generous understanding of forgiveness is rooted in the Orthodox sense that God truly wants everyone to live in loving relationship with Him (see 1 Timothy 2:4). St. John Chrysostom says, "If it were his alone, all men would have been saved and would have come to a knowledge of the truth."[50] The apostle Peter says, "[God] is patient with you, not wanting anyone to perish, but everyone to come to repentance" (2 Peter 2:9). Clearly, God's desire for humanity's salvation was universal, and his pursuit of that desire was rooted in relationship, not recompense. It is our refusal of God's expression of forgiveness in Jesus that leaves us separated from him.

From the Orthodox perspective, God's attitude toward wayward humanity is one defined by grace, not by condemnation. This is the inevitable implication of viewing sin as disease rather than crime. The resulting approach is the bedside manner of the physician, not the cellblock demeanor of the judge. After all, the need is one of transformation, not of incarceration. As Fr. Coniaris reminds us, "Grace is the unlimited pouring out of God's mercy. It is God's *unconditional forgiveness offered to the unworthy*" (emphasis added).[51]

A moment ago, we revisited 2 Corinthians 5:19. The Greek word in that passage, which the New International Version translates "not counting," is $\lambda o \gamma i \zeta o \mu \alpha \iota$ (law-GĒD-zō-mī), and it means that any and all reckoning is ceased. It is not that the transgression is gone or that it was compensated, but simply that it is no longer considered. This is the true meaning of God's forgiveness. The psalmist wrote, "For as high as the heavens are above the earth, so great is his love for those who fear him; as far as the east is from the west, so far has he removed our transgressions from us" (Psalm 103:11–12).

This forgiveness is rooted in God's love. God loved us too much to let us perish in our sin, so he undertook a rescue mission that, to the outside observer, seems strange indeed. As on writer put it:

> A child is born in an obscure village. He is brought up in another obscure village. He works in a carpenter shop until he is thirty, and then for three brief years is an itinerant preacher, proclaiming a message and living a life. He never writes a book. He never holds an office. He never raises an army. He never has a family of his own. He never owns a home. He never goes to college. He never travels two hundred miles from the place where he was born. He gathers a little group of friends about him and teaches them his way of life. While still a young man, the tide of popular feeling turns against him. One denies him; another betrays him. He is turned over to his enemies. He goes through the mockery of a trial; he is nailed to a cross between two thieves, and when dead is laid in a borrowed grave by the kindness of a friend.[52]

This is not exactly a textbook strategy for conquering the world!

In a speech to the House of Commons on November 11, 1947, British Prime Minister Winston Churchill commented that "Democracy is the worst form of government, except for all those other forms that have been tried from time to time."[53] Truly, God's plan of redemption was the worst possible way to save the world, except for all the others! And it sprang from his heart of forgiveness.

Wrath

There is one last misunderstood concept I wish to examine, and that is the attribute we know as wrath. This topic is especially important given the punitive mindset the Western church has adopted with respect to human sin. From the Scriptures, it is quite clear that wrath is one of God's attributes. In fact, in some circles it seems to be God's primary attribute. Certainly, when it comes to most religions, wrath is almost always a staple component. Most world religions (at least those that worship a god or gods) are rooted in the belief that their deity is angry and must be appeased. The nature of that appeasement is often graphic and even bloody. Unfortunately, many Christians also seem to view the God of the Bible in the same way. Still, the fact of God's wrath cannot be denied.

So, exactly what is the nature of God's wrath? Is wrath just another word for anger that must somehow be appeased lest it boil over and wreak havoc upon us? If this is the case, how does this volatile understanding of God's wrath square with our previous discussion of his universal extension of forgiveness?

The Scriptures clearly teach the reality of God's wrath and our liability to it:

> As for you, you were dead in your transgressions and sins, in which you used to live when you followed the ways of this world and of the ruler of the kingdom of the air, the spirit who is now at work in those who are disobedient. All of us also lived among them at one time, gratifying the cravings of our sinful nature and following its desires and thoughts. Like the rest, we were by nature objects of wrath.
>
> —Ephesians 2:1–3

For most of us, the fact that we are objects of God's wrath comes as no surprise. Anyone who attends church even occasionally has most likely heard the assertion that

God is angry with each person's sin and that his anger must be assuaged before a person can, again, have intimate fellowship with him. For most of us, this wrathful reaction to our offense makes perfect sense because it is precisely how we react when others offend us in some way. We get angry and strengthen our resolve that the other person had better make it right if he or she wants to have anything further to do with us. I don't have to search long in my database of the past to find personal examples of such behavior.

I remember a time early in my marriage when I did something that offended my wife. I, on the other hand, didn't think I had done anything even remotely deserving an apology on my part. In fact, I thought she was making much ado about nothing, so I made up my mind that I was not going to tell her I was sorry. The result was an icy quiet that pervaded the house for days. She was hurt, and I was prideful and stubborn. Finally, when I could take it no longer, I caved in and gave her the apology she deserved—one that I should have made as soon as I knew I had offended her.

Offense—even just the perception of it (if one *feels* offended, he or she *is* offended—one's perception is, after all, one's reality)—breaks relationship and stokes anger. The offending party must address the matter if relationship is to be restored. That's the way we human beings do things. However, is it fair to assign such human pettiness to God? We know we are created in God's image, but is it accurate to create him in ours? And when Scripture speaks of us as objects of wrath, is it really painting a picture of an angry deity poised to tee off on his helpless creatures if they don't bend the knee and cry, "Uncle!"? Or is there something else, something deeper at work here?

As previously mentioned, this notion of angry retribution is precisely the understanding of most of the world's

Reorientation

religions in terms of God's response to human offense. Unfortunately, this notion has frequently found a home in Christianity as well. On July 8, 1741, Jonathan Edwards, a Puritan Congregationalist minister, preached a sermon in Enfield, CT, entitled "Sinners in the Hands of an Angry God." In this sermon, Edwards paints a vivid word picture of an angry, even vengeful God dangling hapless sinners over the consuming fires of hell.

> The God that holds you over the pit of hell, much like one holds a spider or some loathsome insect over the fire, abhors you and is dreadfully provoked: his wrath towards you burns like fire; he looks upon you as worthy of nothing else, but to be cast into the fire; he is of purer eyes than to bear to have you in his sight; you are ten thousand times more abominable in his eyes than the most hateful venomous serpent is in ours. You have offended him infinitely more than ever a stubborn rebel did his prince; and yet it is nothing but his hand that holds you from falling into the fire every moment. It is to be ascribed to nothing else that you did not go to hell the last night; that you suffered to awake again in this world, after you close your eyes to sleep. And there is no other reason to be given, why you have not dropped into hell since you arose in the morning, but that God's hand has held you up. There is no other reason to be given why you have not gone to hell, since you have sat here in the house of God, provoking his pure eyes by your sinful wicked manner of attending his solemn worship. Yea, there is nothing else that is to be given as a reason why you do not this very moment drop down into hell.[54]

Clearly, from Edwards' point of view, God is angry with us and his anger must be appeased. His wrath is a yawning chasm of fire into which the transgressors are in imminent danger of being dropped by an irritated deity. The effect of Edwards' preaching was, apparently, profound. In fact, the lore of the day suggests that when Edwards preached "Sinners in the Hands of an Angry God," the people sitting in the pews were so frightened by his vivid imagery of oblivion they literally grabbed the backs of the seats in front of them, some even crying out as they sought to avoid sliding down what Edwards described as the slippery slope leading to the inferno of hell. Such was the conviction of Edwards' fiery preaching.

British evangelical pastor Steve Chalke suggests that the gospel preached today frequently bears the fingerprints of Jonathan Edwards:

> Preaching like Edwards' has been all too representative of the portrayal of the gospel by the Church over the last few hundred years, and, by implication, of any popular understanding of the message of Jesus. And though today, for the most part, the worst of this ferocious rhetoric is a thing of the past, the residue of such portrayals of the gospel still echo across the world. People still believe that the Christian God is a God of power, law, judgment, hellfire and damnation. A God whose strapline is probably, "Get in line fast or I'll squash you."[55]

Such preaching is, clearly, both convicting and frightening. But is it accurate? Let's examine this thing called wrath a bit more closely. Clearly, from the biblical account, it is very real and should be avoided at all costs. But is it, as Edwards suggests, the punitive expression of a disturbed deity? Or is there more to God's wrath than just temper? In Romans 1, Paul says that "the wrath of God is being revealed from heaven against all the godlessness and wickedness of men who suppress the truth by their wickedness" (Romans 1:18). If one were to stop reading here, it would seem that Edwards had it right—God is pounding the sinners in righteous anger.

However, if one reads further, a different picture of God's wrath emerges—one that is far more consequential than judicial, one that is far more a matter of result than of retribution. Three times in the remainder of Romans chapter one, Paul teaches that the revelation of God's wrath takes the form of consequences rather than judgment. In verse twenty-four Paul says, "God gave them over in the sinful desires of their hearts to sexual impurity." In verse twenty-six he says, "God gave them over to shameful lusts." And then in verse twenty-eight Paul says a third time, "God gave them over to a depraved mind, to do what ought not to be done."

In each of these three examples, the revelation of God's wrath was expressed in his "[giving] them over" to the consequences of their sinful behavior. In no sense is this revelation of God's wrath punitive; rather, it is innately consequential. It is what naturally occurs when humanity brazenly assumes the mantle of self-determination. This gives new clarity to Paul's declaration that "the *wages* of sin is death" (Romans 6:23, emphasis added). God allows humanity to experience the natural outcome of their self-determination, which is in direct contrast to their very design as creatures intended to live life in dependency upon their Creator.

The word "wrath" occurs 197 times in 190 verses in the NIV, and God's wrath is clearly unpleasant, even, on occasion, violent. But there is nothing in any of those verses that mitigates a consequential understanding of God's wrath. The judicial understanding many now hold is a conditioned response shaped by our understanding of our own selfish nature (which we superimpose upon God) and by our tendency to see God's main focus as the preservation of justice. However, this all changes when we adopt a relational center for our examination of the atonement.

During the 1930s and '40s, a group of Christian scholars connected with Oxford University met regularly to discuss literature and to critique each other's work in the literary field. Among the members of this august all-male group, known as "The Inklings," were C. S. Lewis, J. R. R. Tolkien, and Charles Williams. Another writer—a friend of Lewis and Williams—who apparently achieved honorary Inkling membership status, though female, was mystery writer Dorothy L. Sayers.

The genius behind the Lord Peter Wimsey series of mystery novels as well as numerous other such works, Sayers, like Lewis, Williams, and Tolkien, was also a theologian in her own right. One of her best-known nonfictional works is entitled *The Mind of the Maker*. Therein, Dorothy Sayers succinctly illustrates the consequential nature of God's wrath:

> There is a difference between saying, "If you hold your finger in the fire you will get burned" and saying "if you whistle at your work I shall beat you, because the noise gets on my nerves." The God of the Christian is too often looked upon as an old gentleman of irritable nerves who beats people for whistling.[56]

Sayers goes on to suggest that this skewed perception results when one confuses the consequences of violating God's natural laws with the judgments pronounced upon those who violate his statutes. Sayers continues, "But today, we understand more about the mechanism of the universe... Defy the commandments of the natural law, and the race will perish in a few generations; co-operate with them, and the race will flourish for ages to come."[57]

Reorientation

Simply put, Sayers (like Paul) tells us that our lives were designed to be fueled by God. If we fill ourselves up with him and live our lives according to his design standards, our lives will go well. However, if we decide to go against the "manufacturer's" specification and fuel our lives on something else—something like "self," then we will experience the natural result of a life operated out of specification. Simply put, our lives will not go well.

We understand this logic when it comes to tangible things like automobiles. If my car is designed to run on gasoline, I wouldn't think of pouring a soft drink into the tank instead of gas. If, in a moment of peculiar rebellion, I were to do something so foolish, I should not be surprised when my car's engine started coughing and missing before finally dying completely and leaving me stranded on the roadside. My freeway distress would, in no way, result from anger on the part of the manufacturer. It would be, quite simply, a result of my operating the car in a way that violated its design constraints. In the same way, when my life sputters and dies because I have chosen to fuel it on self rather than on God, its demise isn't a result of the fact that God is mad at me. It fails, simply, because I chose to operate it in a way that violated its design.

Unfortunately, many in the Western (and, in particular, the American) church have been indoctrinated with the more punitive view of God's wrath. God is angry and we must find a way to calm him down. In so doing, we have equated sin with those imprisoned in its clutches, we have robbed the gospel of its grace, and we have reduced Christianity from the beauty of a loving relationship to the sterility of the same appeasement motif that is part and parcel of every other religion in the world.

We have also grossly miscaricatured God's love. One of Christendom's greatest living theologians, the Rt. Rev.

Dr. N. T. Wright, Anglican Bishop of Durham, weighs in on this very issue:

> We must of course grant that many Christians have spoken, in effect, of the angry God upstairs and the suffering Jesus placating him. Spoken? They've *painted* it: many a mediaeval altarpiece, many a devotional artwork, have sketched exactly that...You'd have thought people would notice this flies in the face of John's and Paul's deep-rooted theology of the love of the triune God: not "God was so angry with the world that he gave us his Son" but "God so *loved* the world that he gave us his Son." That's why, when I sing that interesting recent song "in Christ alone my hope is found," and we come to the line, "And on the cross, as Jesus died, the wrath of God was satisfied," I believe it's more deeply true to sing "the *love* of God was satisfied."[58]

In my church, whenever we sing this song, I make the substitution Bishop Wright suggests (and publicly note my change—I do not believe in altering the works of others without so noting), for truly it is the love of God that must be satisfied. When Jesus took the sin of the world upon his shoulders, removing both it and the carnage it represents, God was satisfied that the object of his love was protected, that we need never be under sin's dominion again.

Commenting on a painting by Rembrandt entitled "The Return of the Prodigal," Steve Chalke illustrates the father's focus on restoration rather than restitution—on relationship rather than wrath. The painting depicts a scene out of the story of the Prodigal Son recorded in Luke 15. The painting portrays not the arrogance of the son's departure or the brokenness of his return, but the embrace of the father, who is overjoyed that his wayward son has come home. Chalke notes, "It is often said that there is a God-shaped hole in our hearts. It would not be unreasonable to suggest that Jesus, by telling this story of the son who breaks his father's heart, is declaring that there is a people-shaped hole in the heart of God. As Henri Nouwen wrote in his classic book, *The Return of the Prodigal Son*:

> He has no desire to punish [people]. They have already been punished excessively by their own inner and outward waywardness. The Father wants simply to let them know that the love they have searched for in such distorted ways has been, is, and always will be there for them.[59]

It is this love of the Father, communicated through decisive forgiveness expressed in Jesus, that frees us from the effects of God's consequential wrath. However, it is not freedom for freedom's sake, but for the express purpose of restoring what was lost through our sin—intimate relationship with the Father. We now turn our attention to the "mechanics" of that restoration.

Reflection Questions

1. What is meant by "reconciliation"?

2. What is meant when we say that forgiveness is universal? How is this different from universalism, which suggests that everyone will be saved?

3. Forgiveness has two components—what are they? Explain how they complement each other and how they are different.

4. We have suggested that forgiveness isn't purchased or compensated. How does this affect your understanding of God's forgiveness of us in Christ?

5. Prior to beginning our journey together, how would you have described God's wrath? Is the suggestion that God's wrath is consequential rather than judicial a new concept for you? How do you react to that suggestion?

6. Steve Chalke suggests that God's focus is restoration rather than restitution. Do you agree? Why or why not?

Chapter 3

Redemption

Behold how many thousand still are lying bound in the darksome prison house of sin, with none to tell them of the Saviour's dying, or of the life He died for them to win. Publish glad tidings; tidings of peace, tidings of Jesus, redemption and release.

"O Zion, Haste"
—Mary A. Thomson, 1878

God and "Green Stamps"

MY FIRST EXPOSURE to the word "redemption" took place when I was just a child growing up in a suburb of Nashville, Tennessee. My mother collected what were in those days called "green stamps." Green stamps were adhesive-backed stickers that were produced in perforated sheets and were given away by grocery stores as a sort of rebate for grocery purchases. The more groceries you bought, the more green stamps you received. I used to enjoy going grocery shopping with my mother just so I could come home afterward and dutifully place all the green stamps in the little booklets that were provided for their accumulation. After so many of these little paper-backed booklets were filled, they could be taken to a Green Stamp Redemption Center and exchanged for merchandise.

I can still remember sitting at the kitchen table and poring over the Green Stamp Catalog. Much like a catalog from Sears or J. C. Penney's, the Green Stamp organization produced a catalog full of enticing merchandise; but it was priced in green stamps rather than in dollars. It was through my green stamp experience that I learned what it means to redeem something. Most especially, it has helped me to understand God's redemption of the human race. Redemption was a magical concept when I encountered it as a child, but that childhood wonder pales in comparison to my childlike wonder now as I consider the miracle of God offering himself so that I might become his once again.

I label my current level of amazement "childlike" because the wonder of God's redemption has always been beyond my comprehension. If my reading is any indication, others have trouble explaining it, too! Perhaps this difficulty with the profundity of his work was what Jesus had in mind when he said we had to come to him as little children. Approaching God as a child is almost a given when it comes to our understanding of redemption, for there is, perhaps, no work of God that is more awe-inspiring than his saving work in Christ on our behalf. From what the Bible tells us, this bewilderment we experience isn't restricted to humanity. The apostle Peter notes that in light of the "sufferings of Christ and the glories that would follow...even angels long to look into these things" (1 Peter 1:11–12). Clearly, when we marvel at God's redemption of humanity in Christ, we are in good company, for even the hosts of heaven are scratching their heads!

Redemption

Earlier we discussed the Greek root for the English word "ransom" ($\lambda v \tau \rho o v$). According to the *Theological Dictionary of the New Testament,* this same Greek word group is "a significant term for redemption in the New Testament."[60] "Redeem" (the noun form is "redemption") simply means to buy or purchase back (the green stamp folks had it right—we were exchanging the stamps for the equivalent value of money we had already paid in grocery purchases). In Christian terms, redemption refers specifically to God's buying back something he once possessed—namely us! Hymn-writing legend Fanny Crosby exclaimed, "Redeemed—how I love to proclaim it! Redeemed by the blood of the Lamb! Redeemed thro' His infinite mercy, His child, and forever I am."[61] When we truly contemplate God's redemption of humanity, celebration is the inevitable result.

Let's examine what we do know about this marvelous undertaking we call redemption. In light of Scripture, there can be little doubt that our salvation involved God buying us back. "You are not your own; you were bought at a price" (1 Corinthians 6:19-20). "Be shepherds of the church of God, which he bought with his own blood" (Acts 20:28). "You were bought at a price; do not become slaves of men" (1 Corinthians 7:23). And in the Revelation, the four living creatures and the twenty-four elders proclaim, "'You are worthy to take the scroll and to open its seals, because you were slain, and with your blood you purchased men for God from every tribe and language and people and nation'" (Revelation 5:9). However, the mechanics of that purchase transaction are not as clear. What was actually paid? To whom was it paid? And how was it accounted? Over the years, the answers I have received to these and other such questions have been truly startling, and they reinforce my conviction that this matter bears further discussion.

Redemption and Release

Earlier we discussed God's forgiveness for our betrayal. I proposed that this forgiveness was extended as an act of his will and was offered universally. However, the universal extension of forgiveness does not imply universal embrace. As the Scriptures also make clear, only some people are willing to surrender the perceived control of their lives, confess their sin, cast themselves upon the mercy of the Savior, and accept his offer of reconciliation. The others will remain separated from God forever.

However, even a desire for reconciliation is not enough to make it happen—one also must be able to respond. As long as humanity remained in bondage to sin, they were unable to embrace God's universal offer of renewed intimacy. By way of example, let us say a man becomes angry and, in a fit of rage, strikes his wife. Hearing the ruckus, a neighbor calls the police. The man is then arrested for assault. Sitting in his jail cell, his anger having cooled a bit, he is conscience-stricken over what he has done. Distraught, he calls his wife on the phone, sincerely apologizes, and begs his wife to forgive him. Since they have been married many years without incident (and, perhaps, because she has invested so much in him!), and since he seems truly sincere and repentant, she extends him the forgiveness he requests. However, that forgiveness on her part does not put everything back neatly where it was, for, we must remember, her husband is still in jail!

Because the officers on the scene determined there was probable cause to conclude an assault under the law had been committed, as agents of the state, they took the man into custody. The charges that were subsequently filed against him were not filed by his wife but by the state. It is the state that is now keeping him incarcerated. His wife may call the prosecutor and plead for leniency on his behalf. She might even go so far as to claim she had exaggerated her initial report or even imply she made the whole thing up (this is not uncommon in the case of battered spouses). However, because the arresting officers found probable cause for arrest, the case will probably proceed to trial. Depending on the perceived severity of the incident, the husband could very well remain locked up until his hearing. Even though his wife has forgiven him, he is still behind bars and unable to pursue the restored relationship she offers. That freedom will not come until something (either acquittal, payment of fine, or sentence served) releases him from incarceration.

The same criteria govern our ability to respond to God's offer of forgiveness. Even though we have been forgiven by the one against whom the offense was perpetrated, we are still incarcerated by the one who gained control over us by our offense. Until the requirements for our release from incarceration are satisfied, we are not in a position to respond to God's forgiveness and his offer of reconciliation.

I believe the early church fathers were right in their assessment that through the betrayal of sin, Satan acquired certain rights over us—rights we gave him by virtue of our indenturing ourselves to him through our sin. That is why the New Testament language concerning the effect of sin is so peppered with terminology like "slavery" and "bondage," while the response offered by God is described as "ransom" and our current word of choice: "redemption." Clearly, in our imprisoned state, humanity was in a situation from which they were powerless to extract themselves. We were in a predicament only God himself could address. The answer to our bondage was Jesus, the Christ. Even his name bears witness to our captive status, for the name "Jesus" means, literally, "God saves" or "God to the rescue."

If our need had simply been for more resolve in licking the problem, God's Son might have borne a name interpreted as "God, the encourager" or "God, the helper." If our need had merely been for an effective role model, his name might have been (as our friend Abelard might suggest) "God, the example." Or, if our need had been for more information—for a better understanding of our predicament, his name might have been "God, the teacher." Given our current love affair in this country with education, this last notion seems tailor-made for our particular situation in the US. I have heard many suggest education is, indeed, sufficient for all the ills of society. If we have a particular problem (e.g., drugs, alcohol, AIDS, etc.), all that is needed is training in what the right response should be. After all, if people know the right thing to do, they will certainly do it!

My experience as a pastor has taught me, however, that ignorance is usually not the problem. More often than not, an individual's wrongdoing is not an ignorance issue. I should stop at this point and clarify that when I say "wrongdoing," I am speaking of doing wrong from God's point of view—of violating his standards of behavior. Otherwise, wrongdoing becomes relativistic—a particular behavior is right or wrong depending upon who it is making the assessment.

No, when it comes to disobeying God's commands, humanity's wrongdoing is usually not a case of something we do not know. Rather, the problem is that we don't like what we *do* know! The reality is, we are far more informed than we are obedient. I suspect the world would be a far better place if folks simply did right to the extent they already know what right is. We already know enough to effect wholesale change, if we want to!

The Bible seems to back up my assessment that our wrongdoing is a problem of the will, not of the intellect. The Scriptures illustrate that Adam and Eve did not fall because they didn't know what God wanted but because there was something else they desired even more than what God wanted. They wanted control and self-determination. They wanted to sit in the big chair. That's why Satan's offer of forbidden fruit to this first couple was worded as it was: "For God knows that when you eat of it your eyes will be opened, and you will be like God" (Genesis 3:5). "You will be like God..." The enticement is just as anesthetizing today as it ever was.

It was because of our pursuit of self-determination that we found ourselves over our heads in a situation we could not even begin to handle. So it is that we found ourselves under the control of one who proved to be far less concerned about our welfare than he initially seemed in the garden. So it is that we found ourselves outside that garden and looking in, confined to a prison cell from which no amount of education or encouragement or self-help training could ever extricate us. So it is that we found ourselves separated from the intimacy with our Creator we were designed to enjoy. And so it is we found ourselves (and continue to find ourselves) crying out to a Savior with no less a name than "God to the rescue," for that was precisely the kind of assistance we needed—and need.

The incarnation was indeed a rescue mission. It was God coming in person to save us from the mess into which we had gotten ourselves—a mess we were powerless to address, a mess that was literally holding us captive. The first objective in this rescue mission was securing our freedom. For, as we previously discussed, before we can respond to God's forgiveness and his offer of restored fellowship with him, we must be free to do so.

As discussed earlier, the idea that Satan was the owner of our souls was prevalent among early believers. We were, in fact, his property, not through attack and conquest but through allure and seduction. Our sin made us the property of the evil one. Earlier, we discussed those in Old Testament days who sold themselves into servitude. Perhaps they incurred debt they couldn't repay, or perhaps they saw potential for a lifestyle in their master's household that was better than anything they could secure for themselves. Whatever the reason, these individuals were, for all intents and purposes, slaves of the one to whom they sold themselves. The only means of extricating themselves from that slavery was either by serving out their agreed-upon term of service, or by having someone else pay the purchase price for their release.

So it is that we, thinking the evil one offered a better opportunity than our previous master, decided to shift our loyalty to a different monarch. We turned our back on our Creator and instead pledged our allegiance to his arch enemy. Too late, we discovered that our new arrangement was not all it was cracked up to be, for our new master offered bondage rather than freedom, death rather than life. Unfortunately, we were powerless to do anything about it.

Had we been kidnapped, God would have been quite justified in riding to the rescue. In a scene reminiscent of many B-grade Westerns, he could have charged into the enemy's camp, subdued the evil one, and spirited us away to safety. However, our willing enrollment in the enemy's service complicated things a bit. Because we entered into bondage of our own free will, God was subjected to the unimaginable humiliation of having to buy us back—of actually having to negotiate with the evil one. And the price for our freedom, the ransom, if you will, was set by the one into whose service we sold ourselves. That awful price was the life of God's Son.

Demeaning Dignity and Surrendering Sovereignty?

Today, as in the past, there are still those who vehemently decry the notion of a ransom paid by God to Satan. It is distasteful to them because, like some early believers, they feel it compromises God's dignity. After all, how could God ever lower himself to pay a ransom to the evil one? How could God possibly find himself in the despicable situation of having to dicker with the devil? The simple answer is, "We put him there!" When we indentured ourselves to his arch enemy, we placed God in the no-win position of sacrificing either his dignity or his beloved human creation. And because he loved us so much, God was willing to take on even the shame of the cross (see Hebrews 12:2) to set us free. The cross definitely compromises God's dignity—and we are responsible for that humiliation. Thankfully for us, in God's economy, love trumps dignity!

There are also those who suggest that the notion of God paying a ransom to Satan in some way compromises his sovereignty. After all, how could a God who is sovereign find himself in a situation where he had to negotiate for our freedom. Perhaps our own human experience of parenting can help us find an answer. In my case, I am the parent of four children, ranging at the time of this writing from age twelve to age twenty-six. I love them all, but my parenting approach is different for each, if for no other reason than their different ages. For example, my twenty-six year old has graduated from college, is married, and is pursuing a nursing career. My parenting approach toward her is almost entirely one of influence since she no longer lives in my household or depends upon me for her sustenance.

My second daughter is a university senior who will soon graduate. For her, also, my approach is mostly influence, although I have a bit of control left since I am still financially involved (oh, am I involved!). However, that modicum of control will evaporate (hopefully!) once she graduates, gets her own place, and finds a starting point for her professional career. Then, like with her older sibling, my role will be one of influence.

My third child, a son, lives at home and is a high school senior. However, given his imminent departure to college in the fall (he is going to school away from home), I have deliberately relinquished the total control that has been part and parcel of our relationship thus far. I am allowing him to make more and more of his own decisions in preparation for his living away from home, all the while standing in the background in case a more intervening approach is required. However, in the big scope of things, my sovereignty over him is also experiencing that inevitable metamorphosis from control to influence.

Even with my twelve-year-old daughter, I am allowing greater freedom. However, I still dictate many aspects of her life—there are still many situations wherein I assert a more absolute expression of my sovereignty. And I shall continue to do so until such time as I am able to release control of her life into her (and God's) hands.

The point is, over time, I made conscious choices to reduce the *exercise* of my sovereignty. For the older daughter, I have released it completely; she is now part of her husband's household. In the case of daughter number two, I have relinquished a great deal of sovereignty since she is now living away from home and is directing her own affairs. As for the younger two, I exercise my sovereignty less stringently as they grow older. For example, I allow my son to drive the family car as long as he does so responsibly. However, I do not have to do so; I choose to give him this freedom. As my youngest daughter enters the teenage years, I shall also begin relinquishing more control of life into her hands, for it is in gradually and intentionally releasing our parental control that our children learn to assume it and to develop it, in turn, for their own children. This entire process is an *expression* of my sovereignty, not a *limitation* of it. At no point in the process was I in any way constrained in the *reality* of my sovereignty, just the *expression* of it. The self-limitation of sovereign expression is, in itself, a sovereign act.

As a parent, this metamorphosis is extremely important, for it is through the gradual, intentional reduction in expression of parental sovereignty that a superior-subordinate relationship gradually evolves into a peer relationship. This is what Jesus was getting at when he emphasized that the relationship he was after was one of friendship, not of servitude. "I no longer call you servants, because a servant does not know his master's business. Instead, I have called you friends, for everything that I learned from my Father I have made known to you" (John 15:15).

God created us from the beginning with free will. It was and is an expression of his divine image in us. God respects our use of that will, for choice is no choice if there is no ability to choose wrongly and to experience the consequences of that wrong choice. Sometimes the choices our children make get them in trouble. And sometimes, helping our children extricate themselves from that trouble costs us, as parents, dearly. I could have avoided the problem entirely if I had merely continued to exercise absolute sovereignty. However, in so doing, I would have lost the growth in relationship that is the goal of parenting in the first place. God created us for relationship, and the relationship he desires with us clearly requires the self-limitation of his sovereign expression. It is a limitation he willingly accepts and even embraces because he loves us.

Those who resist the notion of Satan having rights over humanity also, generally, downplay the notion of human free will, for that, too, is seen as a similar diminishing of God's sovereignty. However, when one looks at the human situation through the eyes of a parent rather than a ruler—of relationship rather than regulation, this self-limitation of the expression of God's sovereignty makes perfect sense. For, as we have already discussed, volition is the hallmark of relationship. God is preparing us to live in intimate fellowship—friendship—with him, the foundation of which is desire. Relationship is unique and special because the parties involved *want* to be in it.

This year, I will have been married to my beautiful wife, Bethlyn, for thirty-three years. Not a day goes by that I do not thank God for his most precious gift of her to me. However, the thing that makes my marriage to Beth so special is that, of all the fellows out there, she has chosen to live with me. It is this volitional aspect of our relationship that makes it so special. We have all heard news stories about a spouse or child escaping from a home confinement in which they were held for years against their will. If Beth's residence with me for thirty-three years was a result of my confinement rather than her willful choice to stay, I daresay the feelings we have for each other today would be quite different!

The same principle applies to our relationship with God. If, as some suggest, God had predetermined who would stay with him and who would not, then the dynamics of that relationship would be quite different from those inherent to a relationship built on free will and on the capacity those with free will have to choose—even to choose wrongly.

From the moment of our original rebellion, humanity has chosen and continues to choose to do wrongly. God honors those choices and the spectrum of consequences they represent, because the only way I really have a choice is if the wrong choice is truly a valid option—consequences and all. The only way I learn to choose rightly is by suffering the consequences of poor choices.

That's why Satan is inevitably part of the picture—he represents all that God is not—the personal antithesis of God's holy character. As such, he personifies evil just as God personifies good. Satan personifies wrong choices just as God personifies right choices. Sin is a decision—it isn't something Satan makes us do. Sin is something he entices us to do. When we make the choice to sin—to rebel, to do life our way and to ignore the loving counsel of our heavenly Father, God respects our decision and lets us depart even though it pains him deeply. G. K. Chesterton once wryly observed, "Hell is God's great compliment to the reality of human freedom and the dignity of human choice."[62] It is truly a great compliment that God would allow his prize creation to turn its back on him and walk away, even to its own destruction. It demonstrates just how special the relationship we were created to enjoy is to God.

I can only imagine how God must grieve when those he loves reject him. Like any parent facing rejection, his heart must literally break. As we discussed earlier, we must come to grips with the reality that we are the ones who put God in this awkward and even painful position. In the Garden, we corporately chose wrongly. We chose Satan as our sovereign instead of God. I personally believe this is why God tolerates Satan—he is the duly "elected" representative of the fallen human race, and to ignore his status as such is really a rejection of the choices we made that installed him in leadership.

In our current world situation, the world tolerates the militant Islamic organization called "Hamas" because they are the duly elected representatives of the Palestinian people. We don't like them because we know they don't represent the mainstream Palestinian community. They foment violence and undermine the very peace process that offers the greatest hope for a bright Palestinian future. Unfortunately, because Hamas appears to be the only hope of having a voice on the world scene (even if it is a violent voice), the Palestinians reluctantly installed them as their duly elected representatives. As such, the nations of the world tolerate them because justice demands it. Had Hamas taken Palestine by conquest, the world could rightly mount an assault and rescue the Palestinians by force. But because Hamas assumed leadership through the willing participation of the Palestinian people, the world can do little but tolerate them unless they do something justifying more stringent action. We are honoring the nascent Palestinian state's right to self-determination, even if it seems determined to go in a way that is ultimately counter-productive for everyone, including themselves.

We see a similar situation in our choice of Satan as our ruler. Because we voluntarily shifted our allegiance to another monarch, securing our release required negotiation, not militancy. The life of God's Son was the non-negotiable price demanded for our release, and God, in his love for us, paid it. This is the essence of ransom thinking—that sin gave Satan certain rights over us; that he demanded a price for our release—namely, the life of Jesus; and that God, in his justice, acknowledged Satan's rights over us and paid the asking price. However, in inflicting death upon that ransom payment, Satan overstepped his authority. Death is the natural result of sin. However, since Jesus never sinned, he was not subject to death, and it was beyond Satan's authority to inflict him with such. Therefore, death could not hold him and he rose from the grave, robbing Satan of both the price and the prize.

The fourth century African theologian Augustine of Hippo described how Satan, in his zeal to hurt God, lost it all: "...the devil found Christ innocent, but none the less smote Him; he shed innocent blood, and took what he had no right to take. Therefore it is fitting that he should be dethroned and forced to give up those who were under his power."[63]

So it was that our release was secured and we were free to respond to God's forgiveness and his offer of restored relationship. Remember, the first element of the atonement was reconciliation or forgiveness: "God was reconciling the world to himself in Christ, not counting men's sins against them" (again, 2 Corinthians 5:19). The second element was release from the bondage that prevented us from responding to that forgiveness. By paying the ransom price, God threw open the cell doors of sin's confinement and made it possible for each and every one of us to walk "out of darkness into his wonderful light" (1 Peter 2:9b). As the old hymn reminds us, "He breaks the power of canceled sin, He sets the prisoner free."[64] So it was that we were forgiven, purchased, and freed for relationship.

"Deeper Magic"

One of the best renditions of this notion of ransom is found in C. S. Lewis's popular children's story "The Lion, the Witch, and the Wardrobe." In 2005, Lewis's fantasy was made into an extremely well-done film, which starkly captures the essence of classical ransom thinking. In this story, one of the four Pevensie children, Edmund, betrays his brother, Peter, and sisters, Susan and Lucy, by succumbing to Jadis, the White Witch's promise of Turkish Delight. Only after he enters the witch's lair does Edmund discover the grass is not greener on the other side after all. Indeed,

Cross Purposes...

it seems there is no grass at all as he quickly discovers he is a prisoner with no apparent hope of escape. Add to that the fact that he is guilt-ridden by his betrayal.

Later on in the story, the forces of the rightful ruler of Narnia, Aslan, the great lion, free Edmund from the witch's grip. He is reunited with his siblings, who are counseled by their feline lord that there is no need to speak further of Edmund's treachery. Peter, Susan, and Lucy, relieved at his return, joyfully embrace him and forgive him completely. For the moment, Edmund's treachery seems to have caused minimal damage. It is soon a distant and past memory.

Unfortunately, to their dismay, the children soon learn that Edmund's restoration is not quite that simple. The White Witch unexpectedly arrives at Aslan's camp and claims, publicly, that more than Aslan's forgiveness is needed for Edmund to be restored. She declares to Aslan's entire camp that the Deep Magic stipulates all traitors belong to her by right and that Edmund must die. Understandably, this pronouncement stuns the entire camp, particularly the Pevensie children. Aslan then holds a private audience with the witch, at the conclusion of which she renounces all claims on Edmund. The White Witch, somewhat reluctantly, even quizzically, departs Aslan's camp without Edmund. There is rejoicing in the camp, as everyone assumes this is finally the end of the matter.

However, later that evening, while most everyone is asleep, we see Aslan steal away from their encampment under cover of darkness. The two Pevensie girls observe him leaving and stealthily follow after him. Aslan senses their presence and, initially, welcomes their company. Eventually he announces that he must proceed alone. Reluctantly, the puzzled girls watch him head off into the forest. Still curious, they find a place of seclusion from which to observe the lion enter the White Witch's camp. There, to their horror,

Redemption

Aslan surrenders himself to Jadis's demonic hordes. At the witch's command, the compliant lion is bound and shorn before being dragged onto a large stone table. There, flushed with the thrill of imminent victory, Jadis gloats over her apparent success. Looking down smugly, the witch taunts her willing captive:

> And now, who has won? Fool, did you think that by all this you would save the human traitor? Now, I will kill you instead of him as our pact was and so the Deep Magic will be appeased. But when you are dead, what will prevent me from killing him as well? And who will take him out of my hand *then*? Understand that you have given me Narnia forever, you have lost your own life and you have not saved his. In that knowledge, despair and die.[65]

And then, with great fanfare, she draws a dagger and plunges it deep into Aslan's royal heart. The crowd cheers; Aslan dies; and the children are left shocked, grief-stricken, and alone. As they emerge from their place of concealment and survey the horror up close, they fear all is lost. What will they tell the others? What will become of the warriors of Narnia who are expecting Aslan to lead them into battle?

The scene is one of gloom, resignation, and despair, for truly, all seems lost. However, their despair quickly changes to fear as a loud rumbling heralds the arrival of an earthquake, which literally rocks and rattles the entire Narnian landscape. When the shaking finally ceases and the dust eventually clears, the two terrified girls discover, to their amazement, that the stone table has literally broken in two, and the lion's corpse is nowhere to be seen. Suddenly Aslan regally appears before them, alive, in all his glory, and their gloom quickly turns to joy.

The children, understandably confused, ask the lion to explain what has just happened. Aslan replies that there is a "deeper magic still which [the witch] did not know...for when a willing victim who had committed no treachery was killed in a traitor's stead, the Table would crack and Death itself would start working backward."[66] Victory is later cemented as the forces of Aslan decisively overwhelm the hordes of the White Witch. She is frozen in time, and all of Narnia is released from her grip. Springtime returns to Narnia, and the Pevensie children are crowned as kings and queens to rule over Narnia until Aslan returns.

In this wonderful children's tale, Lewis captures the essence of ransom thinking, illustrating both the rights Satan had over us because of our betrayal and the sacrifice Jesus offered when he substituted himself in our place—as a ransom. When Satan in his arrogance overextended himself by exacting sin's penalty on one who had not sinned, death itself was robbed of its power and began to work backwards. Jesus rose from the dead, defeating death, hell, and the evil one. Humanity was released from Satan's power and established as "a chosen people, a royal priesthood, a holy nation" (1 Peter 2:9a) until the day of Jesus' return.

It is interesting to note that the words "ransom" and "redeem" or "redemption" occur nearly one-hundred times in Scripture. Clearly, this idea is not just a peripheral concept, even though it has fallen from current focus. It is a concept whose meaning was clearly established before being applied to the work of Jesus on our behalf. I would suggest that the very meaning of terms like "redemption" and "ransom" quickly becomes convoluted if the notion of a ransom to the evil one is discarded. The terms themselves imply both a payment and a payee. The payment is specifically the $\lambda \upsilon \tau \rho o \nu$ payment previously mentioned, wherein a bondservant is freed from his or her master. In terms of a payee, if Satan was not the master, then who was holding us in bondage? And if the payment was not made to the evil one, to whom was it made?

As strange as it may seem, I have heard many suggest that God was the recipient of this ransom or redemption payment. The implications of this suggestion are troublesome. First, one quickly finds his or herself hopelessly mired down in circular logic—in a conundrum wherein God is both the one holding us captive and the one who is setting us free. He is both the one making the payment and the one receiving it—sort of a heavenly version of the old Vaudeville routine where a man pays himself, taking money out of his left pocket and putting it into his right. The funds change location, but never really change ownership!

The easiest way to avoid this twisted theology is to go with the simplest rendering of the biblical text, which in the case of "ransom" and "redemption" means a payment given by a redeemer to a master to secure the release of a slave from bondage. Similarly, the terms "slavery" and "bondage" also mean just what they imply—someone is under the total and uncompensated control of another. As a wise friend once counseled me, "If plain sense makes good sense, seek no other sense." While the simplest interpretation is not necessarily always the best (e.g., we shouldn't take Jesus' claim to be the light of the world as a statement about wattage!), one should start with the most obvious understanding and only depart from it if context or other scriptures so dictate.

We have not always taken such a convoluted approach to the notion of redemption when dealing with atonement. For the first thousand years of the church, Christians were broadly convinced that God, in some fashion, ransomed us back from Satan, the enemy of our souls. Then, in an incredible display of hubris, not to mention ignorance and miscalculation, Satan overstepped his authority and inflicted the innocent Jesus with the penalty for betrayal. As C. S. Lewis so wonderfully described it, death started working backward, and he who was dead now lives. Because of the ransom payment God made on our behalf, we have been set free from our incarceration in sin. Our former evil master has been defeated, and the cell door that held us in captivity has been forever thrown open. We are now free to pursue the loving relationship with our heavenly Father for which we were originally created. Oh, if only forgiveness and release were all it took to live in freedom!

Redemption

REFLECTION QUESTIONS

1. What does it mean to redeem something? In the case of the atonement, what was redeemed? Who redeemed it? From whom was it redeemed?

2. Redemption is the natural follow-on to forgiveness—it allows the cycle of forgiveness to be complete. Explain how this is so.

3. We suggested God places limits on the expression of his sovereignty. Do you agree?

4. Why do some suggest that the idea of a ransom paid to Satan by God demeans God's dignity? Why do others suggest the notion that ransom reduces God's sovereignty? What do you think?

5. What is your impression of C. S. Lewis's portrayal of a ransom. Consider watching the movie version of *The Lion, the Witch, and the Wardrobe*. If you have seen it (or read the book), how did it affect your sense of God's atoning work?

6. The ransom theory suggests Satan lost both the payment and the prize when he overstepped his authority and inflicted the penalty of sin upon one who had not sinned. How does this compare with your current understanding of the reason death could not hold Jesus?

Chapter 4

Recapitulation

What can wash away my sin? Nothing but the blood of Jesus. What can make me whole again? Nothing but the blood of Jesus. O precious is the flow that makes me white as snow. No other fount I know; nothing but the blood of Jesus.
"Nothing But The Blood of Jesus"
—Robert Lowry, 1876

EARLIER, WE BRIEFLY examined what Irenaeus of Lyon called "recapitulation." We saw how his theory was steeped in Jewish tradition, tracing its roots back to the Jewish Day of Atonement, when the sin of the people was exchanged for the purity of the spotless, sacrificial goat. This notion of an exchange of sin for purity is by no means a concept unique to Irenaeus. The apostle Paul employs a similar metaphor in his discussion of God's reconciling work in Christ: "God made him who had no sin to be sin for us, so that in him we might become the righteousness of God" (2 Corinthians 5:21). Clearly when Jesus entered the human arena, he entered it contextually as the sin bearer—the sacrifice for the sins of the whole world. The Scriptures are replete with imagery of Jesus as both sacrifice and high priest. Any discussion of his life and mission must consider these very foundational roles. It was not an accident that Jesus was first announced as "the Lamb of God, who takes away the sins of the world" (John 1:29).

The biblical account of Jesus' life and mission is found in those four New Testament books known as the gospels. The first three gospel accounts—Matthew, Mark, and Luke—are often referred to as the synoptic gospels. The word "synoptic" is really a construct from two Greek words meaning "same view." When the adjective "synoptic" is used to describe the first three gospel accounts, it does so in reference to the fact that all three tell pretty much the same story in roughly the same sequence. Simply put, they offer the same view of Jesus' early life, ministry years, death, and resurrection; although they are written from different points of view and offer different perspectives of the life of Jesus.

The gospel of John, however, is quite different. It says nothing about Jesus' early years, and it concentrates almost totally on his role as humanity's Savior. In reading the opening lines of John's gospel, we detect a mood of impatience on his part in telling the story. One senses John has no time for small talk—the message of God's redemption in Christ is too compelling and too urgent to be delayed. The other gospel writers catalog Jesus' early years and allow Jesus' assumption of his mission to gradually unfold. There is also a certain subtlety in their presentation of Jesus' deity. John, on the other hand, proceeds right to the heart of the matter. And I believe that in so doing, he was declaring in no uncertain terms that Jesus is, indeed, God in human flesh:

> In the beginning was the Word, and the Word was with God, and the Word was God.... The Word became flesh

Recapitulation

and made his dwelling among us. We have seen his glory, the glory of the One and Only, who came from the Father, full of grace and truth.
—John 1:1, 14

In only fifteen verses, John firmly proclaims the deity of Christ. Before even the first chapter is over, John is already describing Jesus' earthly mission of saving humanity from itself, and he does so in recapitulation terms: "Look, the Lamb of God, who takes away the sin of the world!" (John 1:29).

For the remainder of this chapter, we are going to examine the means by which Jesus did and continues to do exactly that—take away the sins of the world.

Expiation

Recapitulation is clearly a two-step process, encompassing both an "out with the old" and an "in with the new" component. The high priest oversaw both the removal of sin's pollution and the restoration of God's cleanliness.

As we have already seen, the mechanics of Jesus' saving work have been and continue to be the subject of much debate. The fact that our only source material resides in language variants that have long since passed from common usage doesn't make our job any easier. Language is powerful (after all, it was how God created everything in the first place!). A single word can literally change the course of understanding. That is certainly the case in our study.

The actual operation of Jesus' atoning work is captured in a single Greek word, ἱλαστηριον (hil-a-STAIR-ion). This particular word appears sixteen times in the Greek Old Testament (the Septuagint) and twice in the New Testament (Romans 3:25 and Hebrews 9:5). In all sixteen of the Old

Testament appearances as well as in the usage in Hebrews, the word is loosely translated "mercy seat" because, in those passages, it refers to the place of atonement. Only one biblical usage specifically refers to the actual atonement operation—to the atoning work itself. In Romans 3:25, the NIV declares, "God presented [Jesus] as a *sacrifice of atonement* through faith in his blood" (emphasis added). The New Revised Standard Version translates ἱλαστηριον similarly. In the King James Version, the New King James Version, the Douay-Rheims Version, the English Revised Version, and the New American Standard Version, the word "propitiation" is used in place of the somewhat innocuous phrase "sacrifice of atonement."

However, if one opens to this passage in the New American Bible or in the original Revised Standard Version, ἱλαστηριον is translated "expiation." Finally, numerous other versions revert to a place description, using the aforementioned notion of "mercy seat." Given this fairly broad spectrum of definitions, one can easily be led to question, "What's going on here?" It's tough enough to understand what is meant when different versions of the Bible translate a particular word differently. It's even more confusing when the English definitions they use in explaining these words make little more sense than the original Greek!

Unfortunately, things don't get much clearer when we consult other resources, such as theological dictionaries. In fact, when I look up ἱλαστηριον in several different theological dictionaries, I quickly discover they display the same spectrum of meaning as the Bible versions themselves. Some of these theological dictionaries translate ἱλαστηριον as "sacrifice of atonement,' some translate it as "propitiation," and still others render the translation as "expiation." What is the correct meaning of ἱλαστηριον, and are these different translations really saying the same thing?

Recapitulation

The dominant view of the Reformers was that ἱλαστηριον meant propitiation. *The Expository Dictionary of Bible Words* reflects this Reformed mindset, defining "propitiation" as "the 'atoning sacrifice' of Jesus Christ. It is this sacrifice that paid the penalty for the sins of the people of God in their entirety—past, present, and future. This substitutionary atonement appeased, or 'propitiated,' the wrath of God once and for all.[67]

Note how this definition illustrates the current theological tendency to see God as angry and in need of appeasement. One is also instantly aware of the editors' decidedly juridical view of sin. This is not surprising given the very punitive view of the atonement emerging from the Reformation. As discussed earlier, this view has sufficiently taken root to become the common understanding today. If you go to most American evangelical churches, you will hear something fairly similar to what we read in the *Expository Dictionary* preached as the explanation of what Jesus did on the cross—that he appeased God by paying the penalty for sin that was rightfully ours to pay.

However, this appeasement view was not at all how the ancient church explained Jesus' work. For the first thousand years of its existence, in fact, until the Reformation, the church of Jesus Christ in the world understood his work in a far different context. As is evidenced today by the most ancient existing Christian expression, Eastern Orthodoxy, the notion of crime and punishment so popular with the reformers was a foreign concept. In sharp contrast to the juridical view of the Reformation, the Orthodox Church maintains a decidedly therapeutic understanding that sees the cross, primarily, in terms of victory, not victimization:

> Where Orthodoxy sees chiefly Christ the Victor, the late medieval and post medieval west sees chiefly Christ

the Victim. While Orthodoxy interprets the Crucifixion primarily as an act of triumphant victory over the powers of evil, the west—particularly since the time of Anselm of Canterbury (?1033–1109)—has tended rather to think of the Cross in penal and juridical terms, as an act of satisfaction or substitution designed to propitiate the act of an angry Father.[68]

    I would suggest their notion that sin needs cleansing rather than punishment is the more accurate explanation, simply because from our relational point of view, it is what is needed. The punishment of crime is intended to have a two-fold effect. First, it is administered as a deterrent from further offense. Secondly, it is intended as the balancing component in a system of justice that seeks to mete out retribution fairly to all parties. The punishment is deemed successful if the offender receives what the system declares as due compensation for the offense committed. The scales are balanced, and the offender is "reset" back to judicial zero.

    However, relationship defies our efforts at systemization. While it certainly seeks to avoid further offense, it does so because of its detrimental effect upon intimacy. As far as fair treatment is concerned, relationship says closeness is more important than fairness. Indeed, when I forgive someone who has offended me, that person may indeed get off scot-free while another offender in another relationship may not be so fortunate. Once again, the focus is almost solely upon relationship. That's because relationship is the ultimate cure for offense. The greatest deterrent to future offense is not the fear of punishment but the possibility of disappointment and estrangement. I can honestly say I have come to a point in my relationship with God where my behavior is governed, not by fear of his retribution, but

Recapitulation

by a consuming desire to avoid ever letting him down. I don't want to do anything that might displease him. Such is the attitude of love.

Recently, I had the privilege of serving as a delegate to a Middle East Peace Conference called Sounds of Hope II (the second such gathering). Sponsored by a group known as Evangelicals for Middle East Understanding (EMEU), this particular conference was held in Amman, Jordan, and featured speakers from all over the Arab world as well as presenters from the West. It is EMEU's hope that Western believers who attend such events will return to their churches with a new understanding of the complexities of the current Middle East situation—one that is not distilled through Western Christian filters. One of the most important things I brought back with me was my amazement at the Palestinian Christians' desire for reconciliation with Israel. This echoed my own personal experience a year earlier when I visited the Mar Elias School in Ibillin, Galilee. There, one of the Christian Arab leaders commented that it was not enough to tolerate the Israelis, for tolerance soon finds a limit. Reconciliation, on the other hand, doesn't merely put up with difficult people; it literally finds oneness with them.

During the conference, I had the opportunity to meet His Eminence Avak Asadourian, ruling Archbishop of the Armenian Orthodox Church. The archbishop, who is normally stationed in Iraq, was able, with great difficulty (and, I suspect, not a small degree of danger), to make his way to Jordan just to participate in Sounds of Hope II. During a break in the conference sessions, I was able to ask the archbishop about his understanding of the atonement and, specifically, about the dominant judicial view. Immediately, without hesitation, he counseled, "You must speak of expiation, not propitiation."[69] Even though I never even mentioned Romans 3:25, Archbishop Asadourian instantly zeroed in on what he saw as the key point of consideration. The focus of Jesus' work was not punishment but cleansing, for that is what prepares us for relationship with a holy God.

I have always been intrigued by the story found in Luke's gospel that we often call the parable of the Prodigal Son. For many years, I read this story without really grasping some of the cultural significance inherent to the story. I am indebted to Kenneth Bailey for the way he helps Westerners understand the many Palestinian nuances of this most amazing and culturally loaded parable![70] One of the things I have noticed in the story subsequent to Bailey's enlightenment is the father's reaction upon the return of the wayward son. The first thing he does is to clean him up! He tells his servants, "Quick! Bring the best robe and put it on him. Put a ring on his finger and sandals on his feet" (Luke 15:22). Gone are the tattered clothes of the swine monger. In their place are the robes of restored relationship. One can also safely assume the servants bathed the dust of the road and the stench of the pigs off the wayward son before clothing him with such privilege. Gone were the vestiges of the old life. A restored relationship was bestowed in its place.

As this story illustrates, there is clearly a need for the baggage of the old life to be stripped away before one enters into the new life—there is a need for recapitulation. This is how an outsider becomes an insider, how a commoner becomes royalty, how an acquaintance becomes family. Restoring relationship involves both removing what separates as well as supplying what unites.

This brings us back to the Jewish Day of Atonement and the process of recapitulation, wherein sin was removed and purity was imparted. In the Jewish frame of reference, it was literally an exchange. At our local home improvement center, I can take an empty propane canister and exchange it for another that is filled. They take the old, empty canister from me and give me, instead, an entirely new canister that is filled with propane. In recapitulation terms, they take away my emptiness and give me fullness instead. In the larger heavenly sense, God takes away my sinfulness (expiation) and imparts his righteousness to me in a process the Bible calls "sanctification"—making one holy or setting one apart. It is to this renewing influence that we now turn our attention.

Sanctification

According to the Bureau of Justice Statistics, 67.5 % of the felons released from prison are charged with another felony within three years.[71] That's because nothing substantive changed while they were in prison. Although they were isolated from the public, the same heart issues that caused them to offend in the first place were still very much alive and well when they were released. As the old saying goes, if you keep on doing what you've always done, you'll keep on getting what you always got!

Nothing changes for us, either, while we are languishing in the prison called sin. The same selfishness that got us in trouble in the first place is still there, even though God has forgiven us. And unless something provokes and empowers us to live differently, we'll soon find ourselves back in the same situation from which we were freed. The writer of Proverbs observed, "As a dog returns to its vomit, so a fool repeats his folly" (Proverbs 26:11). The atonement offers no remedy for foolishness; indeed, the Scriptures give vivid warning of the consequences awaiting those who have been freed from sin's grip only to allow the evil one to re-establish a beachhead in their lives. In his second epistle to the believers scattered throughout Asia Minor, the apostle Peter observes:

> If they have escaped the corruption of the world by knowing our Lord and Savior Jesus Christ and are again entangled in it and overcome, they are worse off at the end than they were at the beginning. It would have been better for them not to have known the way of righteousness, than to have known it and then to turn their backs on the sacred command that was passed on to them. Of them the proverbs are true: "A dog returns to its vomit," and, "A sow that is washed goes back to her wallowing in the mud."
> —2 Peter 2:20–22

The writer to the Hebrews echoes this same sentiment:

> It is impossible for those who have once been enlightened, who have tasted the heavenly gift, who have shared in the Holy Spirit, who have tasted the goodness of the word of God and the powers of the coming age, if they fall away, to be brought back to repentance, because to their loss they are crucifying the Son of God all over again and subjecting him to public disgrace.
> —Hebrews 6:4-6

Clearly, sin remains a problem for even the redeemed. However, its troublesome nature is no longer manifest as a compulsion, only as an attraction. I no longer sin because I have to; I sin because I want to. This is what John Wesley was getting at when he defined sin as "an actual, voluntary transgression of the law; of the revealed, written law of God."[72] We must never confuse mistakes and errors, which are part of normal human limitation, with sin, which is an expression of fallen human rebellion. Sin is something

Recapitulation

we decide to do, knowing that God has called us to do otherwise. It was true in the Garden of Eden, and it's still true today.

Clearly, though God's work in Christ robbed sin of its power over the redeemed, it did not remove its allure. Something had to give us the power to "just say no" to sin. Consequently, God empowered us with his Holy Spirit so that we could stand up against the wiles of the evil one. The apostle Paul, in encouraging his friends in Corinth, referenced this divine equipping when he wrote, "No temptation has seized you except what is common to man. And God is faithful; he will not let you be tempted beyond what you can bear. But when you are tempted, he will also provide a way out so that you can stand up under it (1 Corinthians 10:13).

Earlier, we spoke about how God did not just impute us as righteous—he didn't just declare us righteous in a positional way. Rather, God literally *made* us righteous. Through the power of his Holy Spirit, he literally turned us into what his decree already said we were. Righteousness means putting the world right. Through the indwelling power of the Holy Spirit, I am literally made right—I finally become, in Christ, who I was truly created to be.

My father was a surgeon—a very good one, in fact! His skill in treating breast cancer became quite well known, and he was a frequent consultant to other surgeons in this area. However, his skill was not an instantaneous manifestation bestowed by the American Medical Association. No, his proficiency was garnered over the course of more than fifty years of medical practice.

There was a day when it all began—a day when, after much formal schooling but little practical experience, someone handed him a diploma declaring that he was, according to the law, a doctor. However, he would be the first to admit that he then spent the next fifty years becoming what his diploma said he already was. You see, his diploma made him a doctor *positionally*. His experience made him a doctor *actually*. This is the miracle of sanctification—it is the process wherein God literally makes us righteous.

Frequently in Christian circles, discussions of the atonement focus solely upon humanity's sin and God's treatment of it. We seem to forget that God's entire plan is oriented toward the reestablishment of broken relationship, not the punishment of sin. Sin stands in the way of relationship and must, therefore, be addressed. However, sin was never the point of Jesus' atoning work. He was always seeking to draw wayward humanity back into intimacy with the Father. That's why merely cleansing us of sin is not enough. We must also be reconsecrated for holy living. This is accomplished through the lifelong process of sanctification—being made holy. And unfortunately, in many of today's churches, precious little time is spent on this topic.

Perhaps that explains why, especially in evangelical circles, Christians tend to diminish the value of the *life* of Jesus. We celebrate his birth at Christmas and then race to his death and resurrection at Easter. However, we rarely spend much time on the years in between. I believe that, with respect to the life of Jesus, our friend Abelard was right—he was setting an example for us to emulate, blazing a path for us to follow. Jesus showed us how to live life in the power of the Spirit. And when I say "live," I am not referring to existence—heart is beating, lungs are inhaling and exhaling, brain synapses are firing. Rather, I mean life in all its glory and centered in the will of God, life that is full of purpose and passion. Is that not, after all, what Jesus was talking about when he said he came that we might have life to the full (John 10:10)? In Philippians 2, we find an ancient hymn theologians often refer to as the "kenotic"

Recapitulation

passage. The word "kenotic" springs from a Greek word, κενωσις (ken-Ō-sis), which simply means "emptying." It refers to the way Jesus emptied himself of everything except love when he took on human flesh.

Most of us don't spend too much time thinking about how much Jesus had to set aside in order to live as we do. As an act of self-limiting sovereignty, he set aside his omnipresence (his influence over every aspect of creation), his omnipotence (the full display of his power), and even his omniscience (knowing everything). Remember, Jesus said only the Father knew when he would return a second time (see Matthew 24:36). Only the selfless love, which is the hallmark of his holy character, remained. Simply put, by an act of his will, Jesus lived his life as a human being, empowered only by the Holy Spirit of God.

I remember as a child watching the old television show *Bewitched*. For those of you not old enough to remember it, the show was about a mere mortal named Darrin who was married to a witch named Samantha. Darrin was insistent that Samantha live as an ordinary mortal housewife, and most of the time, she complied. However, there were those occasional moments when mortal life either overwhelmed or simply frustrated Samantha. When that happened, she would, sheepishly, in a moment of weakness, resort to her witchcraft. When she was certain no one was watching, she would, with a wiggle of her nose, invoke her magic powers, and suddenly and inexplicably, things happened that were beyond the comprehension of mere mortals.

Some Christians seem to suspect that was how Jesus operated. Oh, he looked like a man, he walked like a man, and even ate and drank like a man. But on those occasions when he found himself facing larger than life challenges, these Christians suspect that he played the "deity card." Like Samantha wiggling her nose, Jesus pulled some God-sized resources out from under his cloak and the unimaginable happened—deaf people heard, blind people regained their sight, the mute sang, and the lame walked. Dead people even came back to life! When things got rough, such as a crowd that became threatening, he just walked right through them. After all, he was God, wasn't he?

To me, this illustrates an interesting phenomenon—the world struggles with Jesus' deity, but the church struggles with his humanity. In many ways, the modern evangelical church displays some of the same tendencies common to the Monophysites (one nature) of the fifth century, those believers who rejected the decision of the Council of Chalcedon in A.D. 451 that Jesus had two natures, human and divine. The Monophysites said Jesus really just had a single divine nature. In the centuries after Chalcedon, Monophysitism was considered a heresy. Today, it is often just mainstream evangelicalism. It's interesting how all it takes to make a heresy orthodox is to get enough people to embrace it!

The truth is, the humanity of Jesus is hugely important, because his life as a human being literally serves as a roadmap for living our own lives. Jesus lived his life as a human being in the power of the Holy Spirit. The Spirit that empowered his life is the same Spirit God places in the heart of each and every Christ-follower. When we turn our lives over to Jesus, we don't just get *part* of the Spirit or a reduced-feature version of the Spirit. We get 100 % of the same Spirit that God placed in Jesus. Because of that, we should expect to see Jesus-sized results in our own lives. That's what Jesus was getting at when he prepared his disciples for life without his physical presence. He declared:

> I tell you the truth, anyone who has faith in me will do what I have been doing. He will do even greater things

Recapitulation

than these, because I am going to the Father. And I will do whatever you ask in my name, so that the Son may bring glory to the Father. You may ask me for anything in my name, and I will do it.

—John 14:12–14

You see, while Jesus was alive, the indwelling Holy Spirit was restricted to one body, but because Jesus went to be with the Father and, in turn, sent his Spirit to indwell all followers of Christ, the power of the Spirit was multiplied many times over because of all the avenues of expression it now had at its disposal. I fear our problem today is not one of too little Spirit. Our problem is too much "us." The fact is, entire towns turned out to hear what Jesus had to say. Even people who didn't like Jesus had him over for dinner. There was something magnetic about this man; people just had to be around him.

By contrast, we who are the redeemed—who are filled with the same Spirit as Jesus—all too often find ourselves rejected and avoided. When the world saw Jesus, they often ran to him from the hills. But when the world sees us, they often run for the hills. Why? Because the Spirit that was so alive and evident in the life of Jesus is, all too often, suppressed and shackled in our lives. What would our world look like if the Holy Spirit of God was truly allowed to run amok in our lives? What would our world look like if we, as Christ-followers, lived life with reckless abandon, submitted to the leadership of God's Spirit? What would it be like if through the power of that same Holy Spirit we learned to live as true, authentic human beings—living life as we were truly designed to live rather than merely limping along in sin-induced dysfunction?

One of the things we would see is righteousness—the world being made right. This is the essence of sanctification:

God literally "injecting" his righteousness into the lives of his followers. The theological word for this is "impartation," and it is to this topic and a companion topic, imputation, that I now wish to turn our attention.

Frequently, when we talk about God making us righteous in Christ, it becomes clear that the corporate understanding of that righteousness is positional in nature. We are righteous because God has declared us so. This is imputed righteousness.

Before most US Presidents leave office, they issue a spate of pardons. By the mere stroke of a pen, the outgoing chief executive declares by fiat that these individuals, most of whom just moments before were felons and ne'er-do-wells, are now upstanding citizens, free from the threat of penalty or incarceration and entitled to all the privileges of our free society. They are declared free from prosecution because the president says they are, not because any new evidence has emerged to prove them innocent. Their new status is imputed—it is a matter of declaration and of status. It does not indicate that any fundamental change has taken place in them.

The righteousness we receive from God is often viewed in much the same way: One moment we're sinners condemned to spiritual death and separation from God. The next minute, thanks to Jesus vouching for us, we are declared "white as snow." From a positional point of view, this is certainly true enough. However, this is where the notion of recapitulation becomes so important. What God offers us in Christ is far more than just positional righteousness. Because of the power of the blood of Jesus, we are not just declared righteous, we are literally *made* righteous. This is a supernatural transformation that takes place in the heart of a believer when the Holy Spirit of God takes up residence. The same miracle that happened nationally on the Jewish Day of Atonement takes place personally in the life of a surrendered believer. God literally excises the malignancy of sin from our hearts and, in its place, introduces his own righteousness. This is what the apostle Paul was describing when he declared, "I have been crucified with Christ and I no longer live, but Christ lives in me. The life I live in the body, I live by faith in the Son of God, who loved me and gave himself for me" (Galatians 2:20). The old person I was before Christ came into my heart is literally killed, and the person of Christ is given life in me. As a result, the righteousness I exhibit is not just positional, it is ontological—it represents a very real change in my being.

If we hearken back to our discussion of presidential pardons, we can easily see that those who were pardoned are still the same people they were before the pardon. Their status with the authorities was changed, but nothing has been done to actually change their hearts to make them different people. The sanctifying, recapitulating work of God, on the other hand, doesn't stop with mere positional change. The change that God effects through Christ literally changes who we are and empowers us to live lives that are dramatically different from those we lived before—lives that are impossible apart from God's supernatural empowerment.

Through the writer of Leviticus, God declared, "I am the Lord your God; consecrate yourselves and be holy, because I am holy" (Leviticus 11:44). I have heard it suggested many times that this is a target at which we should aim but never really expect to hit. However, I would like to suggest that God is not dangling a carrot in front of our noses so that we will constantly be lunging for something unattainable. I believe God was quite serious when he commanded us to be holy, and I believe he gives us what it takes to make holiness possible.

Holiness means set apart—in this case, set apart for God. This should be the expected outcome of every Christian life. The apostle Peter wrote, "But just as he who called you is holy, so be holy in all you do; for it is written: 'Be holy, because I am holy'" (1 Peter 1:15–16). Clearly, Peter believed that holy living was within the grasp of the believer.

Most of you have probably seen the bumper sticker that sheepishly declares, "Christians aren't perfect, just forgiven." On the surface, this is certainly a true statement. However, it grossly undersells the power of sanctification. On the cross, Jesus didn't just deliver me *from* sin, he delivered me *not to* sin. When Jesus said, "Be perfect, therefore, as your heavenly Father is perfect" (Matthew 5:48), he wasn't promoting some pipedream that lies totally outside the spectrum of human reality. Rather, he was suggesting that we can be perfected (in the Greek, "completed") in him. Because we as Christ-followers have his power at work in us, through us he can do "immeasurably more than all we ask or imagine, according to his power that is at work within us" (Ephesians 3:20). Our only limitation is ourselves.

In his book *The Divine Conspiracy*, best-selling author Dallas Willard introduces a concept he calls "sin management,"[73] that is, the notion that sin is here to stay and we might as well make the best of it. In other words, our work as Christians is to corral sin, to stifle it, to minimize its effect upon our lives. The Christian life is, at best, an exercise in damage control. But conquer sin? Who are we kidding? He is pushing back against the idea that real transformation is only theoretical—that we shouldn't expect to see real change in our lives as a result of our coming to Christ. Reflecting further on this idea, Willard laments:

> On a recent radio program a prominent minster spent fifteen minutes enforcing the point that "justification,"

the forgiveness of sins, involves *no change at all* in the heart or personality of the one forgiven. It is, he insisted, something entirely external to you, located wholly in God himself. His intent was to emphasize the familiar Protestant point that salvation is by God's grace only and is totally independent of what we may do. But what he in fact *said* was that being a Christian has nothing to do with the kind of person you are. The implications of this teaching are stunning.[74]

Once again, we see the focus on doing rather than being that has so emasculated the power and vibrancy of the new-millennium church. No wonder the lives of those calling themselves Christians show virtually no statistical difference from non-Christians in terms of lifestyle issues such as pre- and extramarital sexual activity, abortion, and integrity.

The apostle Paul spends much of his writing contrasting the old and the new life. In his second letter to the church in Corinth, he speaks of how God has "put his Spirit in our hearts as a deposit, guaranteeing what is to come" (2 Corinthians 1:22). Because we have God's Spirit within us, we are counseled to live our lives in a way that is pleasing to God. Paul suggests we literally have the power to do so: "Therefore, if anyone is in Christ, he is a new creation; the old has gone, the new has come!" (2 Corinthians 5:17). When we are born again in Christ, he doesn't just polish us off, clean us up, or even upgrade our firmware. No, he literally puts his Spirit inside of us. Over time, if we allow it, the Holy Spirit subdues the old spirit of flesh and endows us with the capacity to live a life pleasing to God. God literally equips us with the capacity to be holy as he is holy. It is an inside job!

This is an incredible concept, but one that is constantly emphasized in the pages of Scripture. To settle for less is to allow the enemy of our souls to retain a stronghold in our lives. Remember the apostle John's declaration, "...the one who is in you is greater than the one who is in the world" (1 John 4:4). Satan has no power we do not yield and no turf we do not surrender. If sin has a stronghold in our lives, it is because we have allowed it, not because Satan has taken it. This is the power God has given us over sin. He has released us from its grip, cleansed us of its effects, repaired the damage it inflicted upon the relationship we were created to enjoy, and empowered us to live victoriously over it forever. Truly, we can live the Christian life with reckless abandon. We can say confidently with the psalmist, "In God I trust; I will not be afraid. What can man do to me?" (Psalm 56:11).

So, why don't we see more Christians living in this reckless abandon—in this victory over sin? Why do so many believers settle for a life that doesn't really look all that different from that of their pagan friends? Is it, perhaps, because we have taught wrong concepts that have, in turn, produced wrong results? Dallas Willard notes, "We who profess Christianity will believe what is constantly presented to us as gospel. If gospels of sin management are preached, they are what Christians will believe."[75]

As much as I wish to believe otherwise, I fear Willard is right. Unfortunately, in our sound bite culture, we have been trained—believers and unbelievers alike—to allow others to think for us. We let advertisers tell us what we should buy, politicians tell us what is good for us, the media tell us what, supposedly, everyone knows to be true, and preachers tell us what God says. Rarely do people do their own research or even check out what others have told them to see if it is really so. These days, if you can

Recapitulation

say something frequently enough and loudly enough, it rapidly achieves the exalted status of established fact. Just look how fast urban legends become true stories on the Internet! One well-known national magazine runs a feature section entitled "Conventional Wisdom," wherein they track the wisdom of the masses—which frequently proves to be no wisdom at all. In essence, they are telling us what "everybody says." Unfortunately, we who have the truth often exchange it for a lie (see Romans 1:25). Those of us who know better often demonstrate that we are more informed than obedient.

God's Spirit is still at work in the world today. His work is not just in remote villages, where tales of miraculous healings and spontaneous delivery from demons seem far more commonplace than in the halls of American academia or corporate boardrooms. The truth is, God's Spirit is still working, and that work is just as effective and just as pervasive as ever. The question is whether or not I will allow God's Spirit to work in me. Will I allow the atoning work of Christ to carry through to completion, namely, by empowering me to live a transformed life and by provoking me to, indeed, live it? There is still no greater testimony of God's power than a transformed human life. It is the end product of a process that began before the foundation of the world.

Reflection Questions

1. Contrast expiation and propitiation.

2. What is the role of appeasement in the Christian faith?

3. What is sanctification? How does it relate to salvation?

4. Why is the life of Jesus important for us to study?

5. What does Dallas Willard mean by "sin management"? How does this idea relate to sanctification?

6. What is the difference between imputed righteousness and imparted righteousness?

Chapter 5

Resolution

Jesus sought me when a stranger, wandering from the fold of God; He, to rescue me from danger, interposed His precious blood; how His kindness yet pursues me mortal tongue can never tell, clothed in flesh, till death shall loose me I cannot proclaim it well.
"Come Thou Fount of Every Blessing"
—Robert Robinson, 1757

SO FAR, OUR study journey has taken us from the formation of the early church, through the Reformation, and into the modern era. We have considered the various operative elements of Jesus' atoning work and the potential impact of those elements on how we live as Christians. There now remains the task of assembling everything we have learned into a cohesive and easily articulated understanding that can be shared with others who also need to understand the profound work God has done on their behalf in Christ.

The apostle Peter instructed, "Always be prepared to give an answer to everyone who asks you to give the reason for the hope that you have" (1 Peter 3:15). All too often, we in the church are ill prepared to share the saving work of Jesus with others. At least some of that may be due to some of the incongruities we have discussed that are inherent to the current explanation. Hopefully, our time together will equip us all to be more effective in telling the world around us about the wonderful way God so loved each one of us.

Early on, we said we did not want our conclusions to end up as fodder for academic dissection or as theorizing suitable only for mothballing in the stuffy recesses of a classroom or library. Rather, our intent is to offer hope to those people who find themselves, each and every day, living in the trenches of spiritual oppression and depression. Our desire is to provide an answer for individuals like my friend (and, I suspect, like your friends) who perceive a disconnection between the God who is a loving heavenly Father and the God who sacrificed his only Son upon a cross. We want to help them understand just how far God was willing to go to rescue them and for them to truly be able "to grasp how wide and long and high and deep is the love of Christ" (Ephesians 3:18). In the pages that follow, we will summarize our discussion thus far in a way that will assist each one of us in sharing this great truth with our friends and neighbors.

We begin in the garden, where Adam and Eve disregarded God's explicit instructions—instructions given for their own good—and took matters into their own hands.

The Origin of Sin

It is worth taking a moment to consider this "fall" of Adam and Eve (and, by extension, our own fall), for it gives a necessary context for understanding the resulting sin of the entire human race. Earlier we discovered that the word "atonement" is really an abridgement of an Old English expression meaning "at-one-ment." It refers, in our case, to God addressing a relational rift that developed between him and his human creation. The nature of the resulting atoning work was, therefore, prescribed by the nature of whatever it was that caused this rift in the first place. God assessed the problem and devised a response that was tailor-made to our particular situation.

We understand this notion of tailored response from our own relational experiences in everyday life. We address a physical problem differently than an emotional one. We address issues with children differently than those involving adults. We address minor misunderstandings differently than major relational explosions. We do so because the resulting damage is different in these diverse circumstances, and it requires an equally diverse remedy. Most of us can understand that the relational separation resulting from a minor incident is significantly less serious than the potentially gaping chasm created by a major relational wound. So it is that God brought a custom-designed solution to the problem of human estrangement.

In the case of humanity's ruptured relationship with God, the Bible teaches us that our sin—our jettisoning of God's leadership in favor of self-direction—is what fractured our fellowship. In the very first book of the Bible, Genesis, we learn that Adam and Eve lived in intimate fellowship with God and with each other. Each and every day, they met and walked together with God as one would commune with a close friend. However, when they chose self-direction over God's leadership, everything suddenly changed. Indeed, every relationship they had was affected.

Theologian Scott McKnight observes that once Eve was created, "Adam's relations were complete because he has an equal, someone just like him. He now has relations in four directions: Godward, selfward, otherward, and worldward."[76] When the first couple fell, all these relations fell with them. Suddenly they were estranged from God, and rather than expectantly meeting with him in loving intimacy, they sheepishly hid from him in guilty shame. They were also estranged from one another and, rather than living freely and openly in full disclosure, hid their nakedness behind a facade of fig leaves. Their relationship with the world was traumatized to the degree that the earth, which once eagerly brought forth all they needed to survive and even to thrive, now opposes them at every turn. And even their relationship with themselves was damaged as shame and guilt replaced the innocence and peace that once defined them and gave them purpose and pleasure in God's presence.

Theologians call what happened to Adam and Eve in the Garden "the fall" or "original sin," and it is because of this original sin that every human being born thereafter finds themselves thrust into a hopeless situation wherein sin is the order of the day and its devastating effects the fruit thereof. As the apostle Paul reminds us, "Sin entered the world through one man, and death through sin, and in this way, death came to all men, because all sinned" (Romans 5:12). Sin is a pervasive intrusion that affects every aspect of our human existence. Theologian Ray Dunning comments on this understanding that original sin refers to the entire person—flesh and spirit, doing and being: "Humanity is wrong, all wrong, before God, and therefore everything that is done is wrong. It is in this way that actual sin is always an expression of original sin."[77] While different traditions interpret this notion of total depravity differently (the more

Calvinist side of the debate sees total depravity as total in *degree*, while the Wesleyan/Arminian side of the debate sees total depravity as total in *scope*), all agree with the notion of sin as a comprehensive pollution that leaves no part of human life untouched by its defiling influence.

In our individualistic Western culture, the notion of personal liability for corporate misconduct is particularly hard to swallow. From our "enlightened" point of view, we are only liable for those transgressions we have personally committed. From a standpoint of guilt, that is true enough. Through the prophet Ezekiel God declared:

> The soul who sins is the one who will die. The son will not share the guilt of the father, nor will the father share the guilt of the son. The righteousness of the righteous man will be credited to him, and the wickedness of the wicked will be charged against him.
> —Ezekiel 18:20

This passage would seem to mitigate my being declared guilty for the sin of another.

There is a difference between culpability and liability. The word culpability has the same root as the Latin *mea culpa*—literally, "my fault." Culpability is inextricably tied to the notion of agency and free will. In a sense, I am culpable when I am blameworthy—when I am at fault, when I am guilty. However, liability is an entirely different concept. Liability is anything that puts one at a disadvantage, regardless of whether or not that person is culpable. We see such liability illustrated daily as individuals act in ways that affect entire communities. One person can pollute a stream from which everyone drinks or foul the air that everyone breathes. One person can infect those around them with a disease. One person can introduce a concept or an idea that radically changes a nation. And, in the case of sin, one person can act in such a way that the spiritual landscape is corrupted for everyone else. Thus we can say that while we are not all culpable for Adam's sin, we are all liable.

There is considerable debate concerning just how Adam's sin affects the rest of us, and I seriously doubt I will shed much light on this particular matter. However, I will at least review the discussion. Most Westerners describe this spiritual corruption in a genetic sense—as something literally passed down from generation to generation. Theologian H. Orton Wiley calls this predisposition "inherited depravity," wherein all men are "born with a depraved nature":

> The first scripture which indicates the inherited depravity of man's nature is found in Genesis 5:3, where it is stated that *Adam...begat a son in his own likeness.* Here a distinction is made between the likeness of God, and Adam's own likeness in which his son was begotten. Another scripture of similar import is found in Genesis 8:21, where it is said that the *imagination of man's heart is evil from his youth.* Since this word was spoken when there were no other human beings on earth except righteous Noah and his family, it must refer to the hereditary tendency of men toward evil.[78]

Wiley's words clearly illustrate this understanding of sin as a genetically transmitted spiritual disease that is passed down from generation to generation. If you were to peruse most of the systematic theology books written over the past thousand years—at least, those written in the West—you would most likely find some version of this genetic understanding touted therein.

Interestingly enough, however, our Eastern brothers and sisters (who avoided the Reformation with its cultural roots and attendant influences) view the transmission of original sin in a decidedly different way. Rather than something we are born *with*—a spiritual birth defect as it were—the Orthodox believers understand our sin nature as something we are born *into*. They believe that just as humans at birth enter an existing physical environment, they also enter an existing spiritual environment.

The Orthodox perspective is that the human spirit is good because God created it. However, the spiritual environment into which that human spirit is born is anything but good—in fact, it is decidedly toxic. It is devoid of godly communion and is defined by self-determination. In contrast to the more Western notion of genetic spiritual transmission, Orthodox Bishop Kallistos Ware succinctly defines this more environmentally-oriented Eastern understanding:

> The doctrine of original sin means rather that we are born into an environment where it is easy to do evil and hard to do good; easy to hurt others, and hard to heal their wounds, easy to arouse men's suspicions, and hard to win their trust. It means that we are each of us conditioned by the solidarity of the human race in its accumulated wrong-doing and wrong-thinking, and hence wrong-being. And to this accumulation of wrong we have ourselves added by our own deliberate acts of sin. The gulf grows wider and wider.[79]

In short, Adam and Eve's original sin polluted the overall spiritual environment into which our own spirits immediately are immersed when we are born. As a result, we are all adversely affected by the toxicity of this polluted spiritual environment, and our own subsequent sinful living only serves to degrade this spiritual environment even further.

To me, personally, this environmentally-oriented Eastern understanding offers a more logical explanation of the nature of original sin. It preserves the notion that everything God has created is, by definition, good, while also explaining how every aspect of that good creation bears the unmistakable evidence of sin's defilement. Having said all that, I also believe there is a genetic component at work in terms of the transmission of sin's *effect*. Our birth and subsequent life in this increasingly toxic, sinful environment can and does produce genetic mutations, which then are passed on physically. For example, it is a sin-twisted spirit that initially causes people to seek relief in a bottle, pill, or syringe rather than seeking their wholeness in God. As generations of addicts bear witness, that misdirected sense of center can then be transmitted, sexually, through subsequent generations.

Now, in the infant years of the new millennium, we are only just learning the degree to which even emotional dysfunctions, such as depression and compulsion, may be passed on genetically from parent to child. Suddenly, the Old Testament concept of generational sin—so archaic to many modern believers—is proving to be more relevant than previously assumed. The greatest example of the genetic transmission of a spiritual malformation, however, is found in death itself, which continues to affect one-hundred percent of humanity. We are complex creatures consisting of physical, spiritual, emotional, and mental components that are quite integrated and cannot easily be compartmentalized or isolated from one another. An event in one realm inevitably leads to an effect in the others. We constantly see this at work as emotional problems cause physical debilitation or as a long-standing physical issue produces emotional depression.

Resolution

Obviously, this environmental perspective is a natural outgrowth of the Eastern Church's more therapeutic view of sin. As we push back on the whole punishment motif relative to the atoning work of Christ, I find it interesting that the Orthodox do not consider even death to be, primarily, punitive in nature. Instead, they see it as a "means of release provided by a loving God. In his mercy God did not wish men to go on living indefinitely in a fallen world, caught forever in the vicious circle of their own devising; and so he provided a way of escape."[80]

Regardless of the spiritual mechanisms at work, one thing is certain—we cannot separate body, soul, and spirit, at least not during our earthly lifetimes. What goes on in one realm undeniably affects the others. The total effect of sin upon God's human creation encompasses both nature and nurture. It is something we are born into and something we are born with. We can treat that part that is transmitted genetically, to some degree, but only God can treat the part that is transmitted spiritually. Such is the purpose of the atonement.

Earlier, I hinted at a preference for the Eastern understanding of sin as primarily a spiritual environmental issue rather than a genetic one. In many respects, my reticence toward the genetic explanation is largely a logical one, in that the genetic explanation raises questions for which I can see no logical answers. For example, if one can inherit ancestral guilt, why can he or she not just as easily inherit ancestral righteousness? If my parents both came to Christ before my birth, if they were both new creations in Christ when I was conceived, then why wasn't I the spiritual beneficiary of their righteousness in Christ? Why wasn't their righteousness imparted to me in the same way the sinfulness of a lost couple is, supposedly, imparted to a child they conceive?

Then, there is the genetic issue of Jesus himself. The Bible says Jesus was born without sin (see Hebrews 4:15). How was this possible if he carried Mary's DNA? From the genealogy in Luke's gospel (presumably tracing Jesus' ancestry through Mary's line), we see that Jesus is a son of Adam, and the Bible says that in Adam all sinned (see Romans 5:12 ff). If all who descend from Adam have sinned, how did Jesus avoid being genetically tainted? The Jews understood inheritance as a function of the male side of the family. This explains, at least for a Jewish audience, Jesus' lack of genetic pollution. However, we now understand that both parents contribute to the fetal gene pool. Unless one invents a means of isolating Mary from her own issue of genetically transmitted sin (such as the Catholics have done via their doctrine of Immaculate Conception), then we are left with the fact that Jesus' mother was born in sin and, presumably, would transfer that sin burden to her son. However, if Jesus was born into a tainted *environment* as the Orthodox suggest, it is reasonable to conclude that his unique spiritual pedigree provided him with protection from environmentally acquired sin.

It remains to be determined exactly what form this pollution of the spiritual realm took when communion with God was broken. Perhaps it is the same sort of problem one encounters in trying to explain or quantify exactly what happens when love dies. We sense the change, we know it is there, but the "handles" needed for examination and quantitative explanation are woefully missing. One thing is certain: sin is a growing systemic problem that continues to relationally infect everyone it touches. "Cracked Eikons (image bearers), when they coagulate into clusters, create conduits for corruption to work and they do so by creating systems that break down equity and love in various relationships."[81] It is this breaking of relationships—upward,

Resolution

outward, and inward—that characterizes original sin and continues to define the spiritual environment into which we are all born and in which we all live.

There is still a great degree of mystery enshrouding the actual mechanism at work in humanity's fall. Besides losing their garden residence, what else actually took place, spiritually, in the lives of the first couple when they fell? We say the image of God was tarnished or corrupted (those of a more Reformed persuasion even say lost) in the fall. But from an operative point of view, what does that actually mean? Personally, I lean toward the notion it was the indwelling Holy Spirit that was extinguished in Adam and Eve after their rebellion. Given that it is this Spirit that completes the image of God in us when it is restored, it is logical to assume it was the extinction of this indwelling Spirit that polluted God's image in which they were initially created. Once that Holy Spirit was removed, its absence allowed the remaining, already rebellious human nature to exert itself fully in unbridled self-centeredness.

I believe the indwelling of the Holy Spirit restores the image of God in the believer. Paul tells us that God predestined believers to be conformed to the image of Jesus, who is "the image of the invisible God" (Colossians 1:15; see also Romans 8:29; 1 Corinthians 15:49; 2 Corinthians 3:18; Philippians 3:21; and 1 John 3:2). However, even the restoration of that image does not change the polluted nature of the spiritual environment in which it must continue to exist. Adam and Eve lived in a pure spiritual environment until Satan convinced them to rebel and, in so doing, introduced defiling sin into the spiritual atmosphere. As Bishop Ware points out, that atmosphere has continued to deteriorate with each passing generation. When God restores his Holy Spirit to us after our coming to faith in Christ, our spirit is renewed. However, the environment in which that renewed spirit must continue to exist is still highly toxic and won't itself be renewed until the creation of the new earth at the end of the age.

As I said, this is just a theory—my theory, if you will. It is not a theory that can be proven biblically. However, it is also not a theory that can be biblically disproven. Hence, I suspect it is destined to remain a conundrum—one of those questions that shall only be answered in the immediate presence of God.

What is clear from Scripture, however, is that the spiritual climate into which humanity is born and in which it continues to dwell was undeniably altered by our seizure of self-governance. It was that rebellion that perverted us spiritually, leaving us with a spiritual landscape bereft of communion with God—a landscape throughout which the evil roaring lion roams, seeking prey. It is to his strategy that we now turn our attention.

The Orchestration of Sin

As serious as the side effects of original sin are in terms of their impact on our lives, they are exacerbated even further by the ongoing campaign of accusation, deception, and undermining that is being waged by Satan and his minions. As we saw Frank Peretti illustrate, albeit fictionally, at the beginning of our discussion, this campaign bears all the earmarks of all-out warfare, complete with battles and casualties. From Scripture we know the inevitable outcome of this battle—in fact, the victory has already been won and even declared. However, there is still a mopping up operation underway, and the casualty count continues to rise. We in the West are used to being on the winning side. However, this is a type of warfare for which our typical rules of engagement do not even begin to apply.

Resolution

The apostle Paul warned that, "Our struggle is not against flesh and blood, but against the rulers, against the authorities, against the powers of this dark world and against the spiritual forces of evil in the heavenly realms" (Ephesians 6:12). Truly, we are incredibly myopic if we couch our existence in merely physical terms. There is a spiritual realm, complete with rulers and authorities. And the prince of this realm is none other than Satan, the deceiver, fallen angel and devil (see John 12, 14, and 16). He is the one who fomented the rebellion in the first place, and he is the one who continues to lead its dying efforts. Let's take a moment and examine his game plan.

Satan approached Eve in the garden in the guise of a serpent and tempted her with the forbidden fruit. When he did so, it was in a way that appealed to her own self-determination and encouraged her to assert her own will over that of the Creator.

> When the woman saw that the fruit of the tree was good for food [physical craving] and pleasing to the eye [lust of the eyes], and also desirable for gaining wisdom [ability to make their own decisions rather than depending upon God's guidance—the essence of pride], she took some and ate it. She also gave some to her husband, who was with her, and he ate it.
> —Genesis 3:6, bracketed comments added

This was Satan's initial strategy, and if the end of the Scriptures is any indication, it has been his game plan all along. In his first epistle, the apostle John warns, "Do not love the world or anything in the world. If anyone loves the world, the love of the Father is not in him. For everything in the world—the cravings of sinful man, the lust of his eyes and the boasting of what he has and does—comes not from the Father but from the world. The world and its desires pass away, but the man who does the will of God lives forever (1 John 2:15–17).

There it is again—the lust of the flesh, the lust of the eyes, and the boastful pride of life—the unholy trinity. Notice that we see this same three-pronged strategy in play as Satan tempts Jesus in the wilderness. In Luke's gospel we read that Jesus was first tempted in his flesh: "If you are the Son of God, tell this stone to become bread" (Luke 4:3). Certainly, after fasting for forty days, the temptation to secure food by any possible means must have been strong. At first it seems to be such a harmless temptation.

Next, Satan appeals to the lust of the eyes—in this case, by trying to seduce Jesus in his weakest human moment with the heady enticement of power. Alone, hungry, tired, and probably discouraged, Jesus is presented with a dichotomy that must have been hard to resist. The gospel account says, "The devil led him up to a high place and showed him in an instant all the kingdoms of the world. And he said to him, 'I will give you all their authority and splendor, for it has been given to me, and I can give it to anyone I want to. So if you worship me, it will all be yours'" (Luke 4:5–7). The tempter, no doubt, figured even Jesus would be hard-pressed to resist the temptation of a quick migration from desert vagabond to world ruler.

Finally, Satan tempted Jesus with pride, taunting him in his physical weakness and distress to assert his deity: "'If you are the Son of God,' he said, 'throw yourself down from here'" (Luke 4:9). Certainly, in light of the enemy's blatant needling, it would have been tempting indeed to set aside his beleaguered humanity and to explode, instead, in magnificent glory.

I suspect the order of these temptations is not all that significant (in fact, Matthew's gospel orders them differently than Luke's account does). What really matters is that Jesus withstood them all in the power of the Holy Spirit. Unfortunately, as we look through the ages, the rest of the human race has not fared so well in the face of Satan's withering and timeless three-pronged attack. Even many Christians who have the same indwelling Holy Spirit that Jesus possessed have failed to draw upon its all-sufficient power in resisting the temptations of the world.

The truth is that Satan is quite predictable. Perhaps the evil one hasn't felt a need to change his tactics because they continue to work so well. Through the powerful allure of self-gratification and self-determination, the enemy of our souls has enlisted us in his unholy following. Too late we have discovered that we are powerless to escape his clutches without God's assistance. Like a fly ensnared in a spider's web, we struggle impotently against the grip of "the sin that so easily entangles" (Hebrews 12:1). That is why God had to orchestrate our release. Unfortunately, though freed, not every prisoner leaves his or her cell. Some choose to remain in a familiar captivity rather than emerging and going forth into an unfamiliar freedom. It is to living in freedom that we now turn our attention.

The Overcoming of Sin

The first step in that release process involves extending forgiveness to all who offended. Sin is always an offense against God, and our sin may have far-reaching effects. Many people in our sphere of influence may be affected by our sin. We don't have to look far to find examples of innocent people negatively impacted by the sin of others. However, even though the effective casualty radius of our sin may be broad, the primary offense is against God and God only.

Speaking to God after his sin with Bathsheba, King David lamented, "Against you, you only, have I sinned and done what is evil in your sight" (Psalm 51:4). In spite of the fact that David's dalliance with Bathsheba wrecked her marriage, sullied her reputation, killed her firstborn, murdered her husband, and resulted in the slaughter of a number of David's most trusted and trusting officers (see 2 Samuel 11:18–24), David understood that his sin was against God and God alone. So God had to forgive David before relationship could be restored. Nathan the prophet announced that God had done precisely that: "The Lord has taken away your sin" (2 Samuel 12:13).

Oh, there were still consequences of that sin, and David suffered from them for the rest of his life. His power was compromised, and his family was a mess. His realm was in turmoil, and even his legacy seemed in jeopardy. In fact, his kingdom continued to suffer even after his death, eventually splitting in two. But the pall of punishment was lifted, and David was invited to return to fellowship with the Father. Because of this, even the consequences David endured were made bearable by the ever-present power of God's love.

So it is that God also has forgiven our sin and invited us to return to intimacy with him. That restoration of fellowship does not mean there will not be consequences resulting from our poor choices. However, as Paul reminds us, "… neither death nor life, neither angels nor demons, neither the present nor the future, nor any powers, neither height nor depth, nor anything else in all creation, will be able to separate us from the love of God that is in Christ Jesus our Lord" (Romans 8:38–39). And as David experienced, even the consequences we continue to face are more manageable because God walks through them with us.

As we discussed earlier, an extension of forgiveness to someone who is incarcerated is useless unless something

Resolution

makes it possible for that person to respond. We were property of the evil one, and he held control over us. However, that fallen status came, not because we were abducted, but because we left the safety of the Father and entered the enemy camp of our own free will. We were not captured, we were captivated. Therefore, God in his justice couldn't just gallop in, conquer the enemy, and free the captives. Instead, he endured the ignominy and pain of relinquishing his own Son into the devil's clutches. He paid the horrific asking price for our release. Then, Satan, in a flagrant display of arrogance and bloodlust, killed the Lord of Life, not realizing that the penalty for sin has no hold on those who have no sin. Death could not hold Jesus because he had not sinned. Rising from the dead, Jesus conquered death once and for all—not only for himself, but also for all who take refuge in him. As the Scriptures declare, "The name of the Lord is a strong tower; the righteous run to it and are safe" (Proverbs 18:10).When Jesus rose from the dead, Satan lost both the prize and the payment. No wonder he works so hard at cutting his losses by stealing as many sheep from God as he can!

At the same moment the Father was offering the Son as a ransom, the Son, as our great high priest, was entering into the tabernacle not made with human hands (see 2 Corinthians 5:1) and offering himself as a full, perfect, and sufficient sacrifice for the sins of the whole world. Serving as both high priest and all-sufficient sacrifice, Jesus offered himself, once and for all, and his sacrifice did what sacrifices always do—cleanse and reconcile the penitent. In an instant, we who were separated from God by the defiling, separating guilt of original sin were reconciled to a holy God. Jesus' sacrificial blood was sufficient not only for the sins that humanity had already committed but also for all the sins they would ever commit. On the cross, it was truly finished!

As an interesting side note, I would point out the word "sacrifice" has the same root as the word "sacred." While our culture has skewed the meaning of sacrifice to mean giving up something we really want, the actual meaning is to devote something to God—to make it sacred. For example, I have sacrificed my paragliding to God. That doesn't mean I'm not allowed to enjoy it any more. It simply means that I have devoted it to God's pleasure instead of mine. And God has returned it to me on his terms, allowing me plenty of time to enjoy my passion, but never letting my *pleasure* become the focus.

I have seen many pilots sacrifice their marriages, their children, and their employment to paragliding—such is the addictive nature of this sport. However, when I sacrificed my flying to God, he enabled me to enjoy it *his* way and, in so doing, also nurtured my marriage, my family, and my profession. He has also enabled me to use it as an avenue for reaching lost people. Truly, when we sacrifice things to God—when we give—it is "given to [us]. A good measure, pressed down, shaken together and running over, will be poured into [our] lap. For with the measure [we] use, it will be measured to [us]" (adapted from Luke 6:38).

When Jesus offered himself as a living sacrifice, he devoted himself to the Father's will rather than catering to his own. Never is this more poignantly demonstrated than in the garden of Gethsemane, where he subordinated his human will to the divine will of the Father. In so doing, he got his life back. As an added bonus, he got the lives of the rest of us back as well! Such is the nature of a sacrifice made to God; when we offer ourselves as living sacrifices (see Romans 12:1–2), the return on the investment is staggering!

Resolution

So we have the Father offering the Son as a ransom to the evil one even as the Son is offering himself as a sacrifice to the Father—a sacrifice that cleansed us of the guilt of original sin and reconciled us to the Father. However, the third person of the Trinity was not idle during this process. While the Father was securing our release and the Son was cleansing us and making us fit for life with a holy God, the Holy Spirit was indwelling and empowering the forgiven, released, cleansed, and reconciled sinners to leave their captivity and resist the ongoing efforts by the evil one to recruit us back into his service. This is the nature of atonement!

It should be pointed out that even though God has done everything needed to forgive, free, cleanse, and reconcile us back to loving intimacy with him, we must still respond to God's offer. And that response requires more than just mental assent to the truth behind God's offer. There is an active component to faith that must not be understated.

The Greek verb for faith is πιστευω (pis-TOO-ō). If one were to literally translate this verb into English, it would read, "I faith." However, we have no such verb in our word arsenal. As a result, we usually translate this verb, "I believe."

> Our English word "faith" comes from the Latin *fides*, as developed through the Old French words *fei* and *feid*. In Middle English (1150–1475) "faith" replaced a word that eventually evolved into "belief." "Faith" came to mean "loyalty to a person to whom one is bound by promise or duty." Faith was fidelity. "Belief" came to be distinguished from faith as an intellectual process having to do with the acceptance of a proposition. The verb form of "faith" dropped out of English usage toward the end of the sixteenth century.[82]

For many believers (faithers!), turning to Christ continues to be a predominantly intellectual process. Perhaps that's why so many Christians who claim the release God offers them in Christ never actually leave their captivity. This is perhaps the most pathetic human tragedy of all, for in so doing, they run the risk of giving the enemy a fresh hold on their lives.

Our previous consideration of Hebrews 6:4–6 and 2 Peter 2:20–22 illustrates this danger. Repentance is something God in his grace permits and through his Spirit empowers. As long as we act on that permission and live in that empowerment, nothing can snatch us out of the Father's hand (see John 10:29). The apostle John counseled his students, "You, dear children, are from God and have overcome them, because the one who is in you is greater than the one who is in the world" (1 John 4:4). Simply put, Satan has no turf we don't surrender and no power we don't yield.

However, if we refuse to act on God's permission and live in his empowerment, we do, in fact, surrender ourselves back into the clutches of the very one from whom we were freed; and in so doing, we repudiate the power of the resurrection. This is what the writer to the Hebrews means when he says we put Jesus back on the cross as a disgraced common criminal. Truly, we have turned our backs on the only means of freedom available to us. This is what James is getting at when he cautions that "as the body without the spirit is dead, so faith without deeds is dead" (James 2:26). Our works are the evidence of a living faith, and anything other than a living faith is just an empty mental exercise.

Finally, the Spirit's empowerment also enables the new saint to live a life that is pleasing to God, joyous for the believer, and fulfilling in terms of God's purpose for them in the world. It is not a life relegated to the mere management of sin—of trying hard, but unsuccessfully, to keep sin in its place. Rather, it is a life of true victory, wherein the power of the indwelling Holy Spirit enables us to stand in the face of the worst temptation and oppression the evil one can hurl our way. As Jesus did when he was tempted with the lust of the flesh, the lust of the eyes, and the boastful pride of life, we too can send Satan packing. Thanks be to God, who enables us to live a life that is truly holy, a God who, as Paul declared, frees us from our body of death (see Romans 7:24).

All of this achieves the purpose for which humanity was initially created, and the potential for which Jesus prayed—intimacy with God: "My prayer is not for them alone. I pray also for those who believe in me through their message, that all of them may be one, Father, just as you are in me and I am in you. May they also be in us so that the world may believe that you have sent me" (John 17:20–21).

It is staggering to realize that Jesus literally prayed that we, as believers, would be drawn into the very intimacy of the Trinity: "Father, as you are in me and I am in you. May they also be in us..." What wondrous love is this?! What power it represents! For it should be apparent that none but the holy may enter such a lofty relationship, and nothing but the love of God can make us holy.

The late Francis Schaeffer wrote a book entitled *How Shall We Then Live?* In it, he examined the effect the power of the cross can have in the lives of the redeemed. "How shall we then live?" It is a question we should all, indeed, ask ourselves. Given who we are without God—poor, brokenhearted, blind, and imprisoned (see Isaiah 61)—and given all God has done to bring us into life-giving fellowship with himself—exchanging beauty for ashes, the oil of gladness for mourning, and a garment of praise for despair (again, see Isaiah 61)—how should we then live our lives?

So again, I return to my friend's comment on that Bible study night a while back:

> Well, you say that God couldn't just sweep my sins under the carpet—that someone had to pay for my sin. Then you tell me God loves me so much that he couldn't bear to see me pay for it, so he punished Jesus instead. I guess I'm not sure I want to be God's child if he would punish another one of his kids for something he didn't even do. What kind of a Father is he, anyway?

The answer is that he is the kind of Father who is not looking to punish your wrongdoing but to free you from it. He is the kind of Father who has chosen to forgive rather than to seek retribution. He is the kind of Father who literally stepped down from his throne and took on the tattered trappings of human flesh, who lived a perfect life as both an example and as a means of cleansing us all. And then, he offered himself in exchange for our release, that we might be reunited with him once again in eternal fellowship. That's the kind of Father he is!

My hope is that our brief journey together will provoke you to live your life with new vigor, even with reckless abandon, and that you will begin to understand the deep, deep love of Jesus and to realize that you are God's precious child. I hope you will come to accept the reality that God is not looking to grade your paper but to hold you close in his embrace. And I hope God's perfect love—a love demonstrated by the offering of his only Son—casts out any fear of punishment. All of this, God has done so that you could be reunited with him. The apostle John counsels us, thusly, in his first epistle:

> God is love. Whoever lives in love lives in God, and God in him. In this way, love is made complete among us so

that we will have confidence on the day of judgment, because in this world we are like him. There is no fear in love. But perfect love drives out fear, because fear has to do with punishment. The one who fears is not made perfect in love.

—1 John 4:16–19

The language of Scripture makes it clear that God is not interested in punishment but in reconciliation—indeed, in relationship.

> The atonement was needed because we are sinners. Sin has subverted our covenant relationship with God. Sin makes covenant relationship impossible because we are unable to meet our covenant obligations... The atonement restored authentic humanity and made it fit for covenant relationship.[83]

Because we have misunderstood original sin, we have been pressed to accept the notion that humanity is basically evil—after all, we're born with a sin nature, and sin is evil. However, the incarnation suggests that we are not basically evil at all. The incarnation echoes a theme that has been ringing through the heavens since the beginning. After the first five days of creation, God characterized his work as "good." After the sixth and final day, when God created humanity, he declared his work to be "very good" (Genesis 1:31). In sending Jesus to take on human flesh, model life in the Spirit, die a reconciling death, and defeat death on our behalf, God signaled that his human creation is still "very good" in spite of being born in a tainted spiritual environment.[84] In his second letter to Corinth, the apostle Paul declares:

Cross Purposes...

> For the Son of God, Jesus Christ, who was preached among you by me and Silas and Timothy, was not "Yes" and "No," but in him it has always been "Yes." For no matter how many promises God has made, they are "Yes" in Christ. And so through him the "Amen" is spoken by us to the glory of God.
> —2 Corinthians 1:19–20

God says, "Yes!" to humanity in general, and he says, "Yes!" to you in particular. When God looks at you, his is not the macroscopic view of the "Where's Waldo?" series of children's books, wherein the reader is hard pressed to find a miniscule Waldo obscured by the sheer magnitude of the maddening crowd. Rather, God's view of you and of me is intensely up close and personal. When God was offering his Son as a ransom, it was your face he saw through the prison bars. When Jesus was hanging and dying on the cross, it was your face he saw staring up at him. When the Holy Spirit was indwelling the ranks of the redeemed, it was your face he saw reunited with the Father. God would have come for you even if you were the only human being on earth. Such is the scope and depth of God's love. The prophet Zephaniah rejoiced, "The Lord your God is with you, he is mighty to save. He will take great delight in you, he will quiet you with his love, he will rejoice over you with singing" (Zephaniah 3:17). Such is the passion of the Father.

In the past, I have preached that God cannot just sweep our sins under the carpet. However, in so saying, I was, at the same time, suggesting there is some system to which even God is subject. I now understand this is simply not the case. For this, in and of itself, is a limitation of God's sovereignty. The only thing dictating God's actions is God himself as expressed in his holy character, and that character is, first and foremost, defined by love. It is because of his love—because he *is* love that God demands justice. However, it isn't justice for himself that he is seeking; it is justice for the rest of his creation. There is no punishment that can satisfy God because there is no human transgression that can offend him personally. That's not to say God is not angered by sin; he most certainly is. However, when God is angered over human sin, it is not because of the personal affront it represents but because of the damage it causes within creation—both to perpetrator and recipient—and because of the destruction it renders to his desired relationship with humanity.

Even God's desire for relationship isn't self-gratifying. Rather, it is focused on blessing his creation—on blessing us. God is love, and love must be expressed. Because God is loving—again, because he *is* love—he wants to lavish himself upon us. Sin is a problem because it gets in the way of the unbridled expression of that selfless love. Please understand that I am not minimizing the catastrophic nature of sin. Sin is a serious business—we know this because it cost the very life of God's Son. I would never trivialize sin. However, I also refuse to trivialize God. I will not, indeed, I cannot, reduce God down to the level wherein there is some human offense, or even a collection of human offenses, that can somehow raise God's royal ire to the point where he must receive satisfaction by punishing someone. Such a reduction overlays human petulance upon a God who, over and over again, proves he is not subject to such human frailties. In suggesting that God's need to punish was even greater than his desire to preserve his Son, we rightly invite such questions as I was asked at that Bible study.

It is also worth acknowledging, once again, our debt to the many great minds of the past who have wrestled with the notion of the atonement, and who have shared their struggles with us. Many of their observations concerning the atonement have withstood the rigors of time, the encroachment of culture, and the litmus test of Scripture. However, I take particular exception to those who suggest that God had to punish someone, so he punished Jesus instead of us. If there is a single element of the current dominant atonement view I would respectfully reject, it is this notion of Jesus as victim rather than as victor. For it establishes the maintenance of some amorphous system of justice as God's overarching purpose in the incarnation rather than the reconciliation of shattered relationship. If nothing else stands out in Scripture, one thing is clear: "... God is love. This is how God showed his love among us: He sent his one and only Son into the world that we might live through him" (1 John 4:8–9). God's release, God's redemption, God's recapitulation, these all are rooted in his love. And they are relevant for us because we, as the redeemed, are the ambassadors of that love in a world that is as desperate to receive it as ever. It is to this relevance that we now turn our attention.

REFLECTION QUESTIONS

1. What is meant by "original sin"? Discuss the idea that it is something we are born into rather than something we are born with (environmental vs. genetic).

2. We suggested Satan's three areas of assault are the lust of the flesh, the lust of the eyes, and the boastful pride of life. Do you agree? How do you see this strategy being worked out in your own life?

3. We suggested that sin is always an offense against God. Do you agree?

4. We said that justice isn't God's primary focus, but that it *is* important to him. Why does justice matter to God?

5. I suggested that God cannot really be offended by his human creation. Do you agree?

6. We suggested that the atonement process consists of a unified activity of the Trinity, wherein:

    - God forgives us.
    - God redeems and releases us.
    - God cleanses and reconciles us.
    - God empowers us.

    What is your reaction to this suggested process?

Chapter 6

Relevance

> *Rescue the perishing, care for the dying; Jesus is merciful, Jesus will save!*
> "Rescue the Perishing"
> —Fanny J. Crosby, 1869

ONE OF THE accusations frequently leveled at the church, especially in this country, is that we are irrelevant—that we have nothing to offer our world that is at all pertinent or of any intrinsic value. Nothing could be further from the truth; however, this is not a new charge.

In the sixth chapter of John's gospel, we read an account in which Jesus has explained the underlying meaning of the Lord's Supper. As you may recall, it was a hard teaching, and some resisted accepting it:

> Jesus said to them, "I tell you the truth, unless you eat the flesh of the Son of Man and drink his blood, you have no life in you. Whoever eats my flesh and drinks my blood has eternal life, and I will raise him up at the last

day. For my flesh is real food and my blood is real drink. Whoever eats my flesh and drinks my blood remains in me, and I in him."

—John 6:53–56

Understandably, there were some who were confused by this notion of eating flesh and drinking blood. The Scriptures go on to report that many turned away and no longer followed him. "'You do not want to leave too, do you?' Jesus asked the Twelve. Simon Peter answered him, 'Lord, to whom shall we go? You have the words of eternal life'" (John 6:67–68).

The world hears what the church has to say today and often turns away, just as it did in Jesus' day. In so doing, they continue to turn their backs on the only one who has the words of eternal life. Our message of hope is just as relevant today as it ever was. However, the task of demonstrating that relevancy is a daunting one. Unfortunately, we who follow Jesus have often made it even harder by embracing a message that, all too frequently, is skewed by the intrusion of cultural influences wherein we interpret the gospel apart from its original context. We take the words of Jesus, spoken to a Middle Eastern first century culture, and examine them through the lens of our own twenty-first century Western environment—an environment that is the culmination of influences decidedly different than those shaping the Middle East. We also have a tendency to create God in our image (rather than accepting the biblical assertion we are created in his), to expect him to act as we would, within human constraints, rather than expecting him, as God, to operate outside the limitations and even the understanding of human creation. When either of these mutations is allowed to influence our message, our news often ceases to be good. This is especially true when we assume God handles offenses like we often do.

Relevance

Recently, a Japanese friend of my wife wrote her with a problem. I shall not identify the friend because I wish to share a portion of her letter (with her permission). Listen to this dear lady's heart as she pours out her pain and frustration:

Dear Beth,
   Today, my dentist decided to extract my dental implant, as he saw no bone growing around the implant. He thinks that he will try another kind to see if it works. I am so disappointed that I waited patiently 6 months and going through the pain. Now I have to go through the pain (physical and complaint from my husband) again and pay again for the procedure and implant.
   I understand that only good things are coming from God and bads are from the devil. Is it true? Or am I punished for whatever reason God thinks I am not doing good? I have been trying my best I can. I am trying to refocus my negative thought reminding it is not from Him, but something else. What's wrong with me?

This woman has been a Christian for many years. However, she has been immersed in and shaped by a church culture that, at least in terms of tradition, emphasizes the punitive nature of God. As a result, this poor woman, who is living with great physical and emotional pain, now wonders if her dental distress is somehow God's punishment for some transgression of which she is not even aware! As a pastor, I encounter people like her virtually every day—people who think their pain and hardship is retributive, that God is punishing them for something, even though they may not even know what it is. This attitude is not unlike that of the Jews of Jesus' day who thought infirmity and disease were directly attributable to some sin on the part of the sufferer or perhaps their family (see the story of the man born blind in John 9). No wonder people find the church irrelevant; they have enough pain, condemnation, and disappointment in their lives without signing up for another dose of misery on Sundays!

However, the church was not always perceived this way. The early church, though lacking in many of the resources the modern church takes for granted, was on the cutting edge in terms of positive public relations. There was a certain relevance to their lives and their message that those around them simply could not ignore. The apostle Luke noted:

> They [the early believers] devoted themselves to the apostles' teaching and to the fellowship, to the breaking of bread and to prayer. Everyone was filled with awe, and many wonders and miraculous signs were done by the apostles. All the believers were together and had everything in common. Selling their possessions and goods, they gave to anyone as he had need. Every day they continued to meet together in the temple courts. They broke bread in their homes and ate together with glad and sincere hearts, praising God *and enjoying the favor of all the people. And the Lord added to their number daily those who were being saved.*
> —Acts 2:42–47, emphasis added

These early Christians lived in a land occupied by hostile foreign forces. They were threatened by the Jews who saw them as heretics and by pagan devotees who saw them as competition. Nevertheless, they had something about them, a winsomeness of spirit, those around them could not ignore. Because of the witness of their lives, thousands of people were won to Christ. So why is a message that was deemed so relevant to the people of the first century judged irrelevant by the people of the twenty-first century? Have things changed so much in two-thousand years? Is Jesus no longer needed?

In the seventh chapter of the letter to the Hebrews, Jesus is compared with the great high priest of the Jewish sacrificial system. In this comparison, however, he is positioned as being even greater than the high priest. In fact, he is compared to a semi-mythical priest named Melchizedek, whose biblical description is sparse at best. In fact, his entire story (all that we know of it biblically) is archived in just three verses in Genesis 14:

> Then Melchizedek king of Salem brought out bread and wine. He was priest of God Most High, and he blessed Abram, saying, "Blessed be Abram by God Most High, Creator of heaven and earth. And blessed be God Most High, who delivered your enemies into your hand." Then Abram gave him a tenth of everything.
> —Genesis 14:18–20

The writer to the Hebrews uses this ephemeral character as a forerunner of Jesus' high priestly ministry. Melchizedek appears with no beginning or end. Unlike Hebrew priests, he was not a descendant of Levi. Indeed, Levi's ancestor, Abram, bowed before Melchizedek and gave him a tithe. The writer to the Hebrews points out that Melchizedek blessed Abram, and the lesser is always blessed by the greater. In fact, given that Levi was "still in the body of his ancestor" (see Hebrews 7:10 for the Jewish understanding of genealogy), one could even say that Levi, who collected the tithe from Israel, offered the tithe to Melchizedek through Abram. The main point in elevating Melchizedek over Levi is to contrast the inadequacy of the Levitical priesthood with the sufficiency of Jesus' priesthood, for the Jewish priests could not remove sin from the people. They could only gloss it over temporarily through sacrifices. However, as our great high priest, Jesus has actually taken our sin away. "Unlike the other high priests, he does not need to offer sacrifices day after day, first for his own sins, and then for the sins of the people. He sacrificed for their sins once for all when he offered himself" (Hebrews 7:27).

Years ago, I had an old Ford pickup truck that was starting to rust in numerous places. I took it into a paint shop to get an estimate. The paint job itself wasn't too expensive, but removing all the rust would have required a second mortgage on my house! I asked the body man if we couldn't just sand the rough spots, paint it, and call it good. He told me that if I painted it without completely removing the rust, it would look great at first, but after a few weeks, the rust would start to blister through the paint. Before long, he said, it would look even worse than it did before it was painted.

Covering up sin with sacrifices was just about as effective. Unless people somehow removed the underlying sin, it would soon reemerge, and they would have to offer sacrifices all over again. Sacrifices were, at best, a temporary stop-gap that only lasted so long. In the end, you were still as far away from God as ever.

Jesus' priesthood was different. Because he offered *himself* as a sacrifice, sin could actually be removed; it was not just glossed over. For the first time in history, humanity had the hope of freedom rather than inevitable damage control.

Our world today is spinning out of control. Just as it was in Jesus' day, the world continues to labor in the sweatshop of sin. The world economy (at the time of this writing) is in a tailspin, largely due to the extraordinary greed of those in positions of power. But it's not just the economy that is in trouble. The following represents just a slice of

Relevance

what went on during the second week of March, 2009: My own state of Washington just approved a bill legalizing physician-assisted suicide (the second in the nation after Oregon). Nationally, the president just rescinded the law prohibiting federal funding of experimentation on stem cells taken from human embryos. A pastor in Illinois was murdered right in front of his congregation during morning worship. A local radio talk show was discussing the pros and cons of genetically engineering children in the womb. And there is, once again, a push to remove "In God We Trust" from our common currency. All of these stories made headlines at virtually the same time, and this was just one week out of the year! Those who think the world is getting better and who claim that human ingenuity and know-how are all it takes to produce a better tomorrow are fooling themselves.

The apostle Paul could just as easily have been describing modern western culture when he lamented over the society of his day:

> ...although [humanity] knew God, they neither glorified him as God nor gave thanks to him, but their thinking became futile and their foolish hearts were darkened. Although they claimed to be wise, they became fools and exchanged the glory of the immortal God for images made to look like mortal man and birds and animals and reptiles.
> —Romans 1:21–22

So, given the similarity of Paul's culture and ours in terms of decadence, why were the Christians of Paul's days seen as having a relevant message for their society while the Christians of our day are often perceived as having nothing important to offer? Perhaps the difference is not so much in the message as it is in the way it is proclaimed. Perhaps, rather than condemning their culture as fodder for God's judgment, the early believers embraced their culture as candidates for God's deliverance. Perhaps they saw those living in sin around them, not as the enemy, but as prisoners of the enemy. Perhaps their message was more about God's desire for fellowship with them than about his anger over how far they had strayed.

Lest I be accused of soft selling sin, let me reiterate that sin is *the* problem of Scripture—it is the means by which "death came to all men" (Romans 5:12). As we discussed earlier, sin is what separated us from God in the first place, and it is still the issue that must be addressed if that relationship is to be restored. We do ourselves, our message, and our world a disservice if we paint sin as anything other than what it is—a rebellion against God, a usurping of his glory, and a lifestyle that is fatal if not addressed. This is the reality of sin, and there will be people who go off into a Christless eternity because of it. To depict sin in any other way is to misconstrue the truth.

However, sin *is not* the focal point of Scripture—reconciliation is. When we tell this story in such a way that God's motivation behind the atonement of sin is a desire for punishment rather than a forgiving, all-consuming, self-sacrificing love, we have also misconstrued the truth. When we do so, we, without realizing it, also have misrepresented the reason God so detests sin.

Earlier we discussed the wrath of God and its consequential nature. That wrath, according to Paul in his letter to Rome, "is being revealed from heaven against all the godlessness and wickedness of men who suppress the truth by their wickedness" (Romans 1:18). Notice how Paul identifies the issue behind that wrath as the suppression of the truth. When we live in a way that declares our own sovereignty, we live a lie, because we are dependent upon God whether we admit it or not. However, when we continue living that lie, fruitless though such an effort might be, we also serve the enemy's purposes as a smokescreen—a living delusion he exploits in trying to lure others into living that lie as well. That's why sin is so distasteful to God. He is not angry with sin because of its effect upon him—he has big shoulders and can take the best we throw his way. No, God's anger toward sin is rooted in the damage it causes within the human spectrum. Sin robs us of intimacy with God, of intimacy with one another, and it leads others into spiritual isolation. Sin causes pain, sickness, suffering, war, pestilence, and death. And God hates it because of all the damage it does.

Another way we misconstrue the truth is by the way we interact with sinners. I have always been amazed at the way Jesus hung around with pretty seedy characters. With great regularity, we find Jesus rubbing shoulders with adulterous women, shady tax collectors, prostitutes, Gentiles, and self-righteous religious leaders. Yet not one of them felt condemned by Jesus. In fact, Jesus never really points out their sin—he lets them do that themselves! It's almost as if the darkness of their sin suddenly stood vividly out against the backdrop of his purity. Jesus never approached them with the threat of punishment. Rather, he encouraged them with the offer of hope.

Someone once commented that it's a bad idea to try teaching a pig to sing—it wastes your time, and it annoys the pig! One could offer a similar observation regarding the wisdom of telling sinners they are sinners. The reality is that they already know it!

The Scriptures tell us sin and guilt go together (see 2 Chronicles 28:13; Job 31:33; Psalm 32:5; and John 16:8 for just a few examples). Sin is the actual offense against God, and guilt is the resulting effect the inevitable estrangement has upon us. Sinners experience guilt, whether they call it such or not. The fact is, if a person is living a life separated from God by his or her rebellion—if that person's spirit is disconnected from the source of its life, there will be a spiritual dis-ease until it is reconnected. Augustine observed, "Thou hast made us for thyself, O Lord, and our heart is restless until it finds its rest in thee."[85] Sinners don't need to be told they are sinners; they need to be told that there is hope for the searing spiritual pain that saps their spirit and robs them of the joy they sense is there but somehow eludes them. This is why Satan works so hard at reinforcing our delusion of self-sufficiency. If he can deceive us into rejecting the truth of our need for God and, instead, declaring our independence from any monarch but ourselves, he robs us of the very sustenance our spirits need to survive. In so doing, he isolates us from our only possible hope of freedom from sin's bondage.

One of the results of the mixed message we have sent—the message that God is both loving and vengeful—is the common perception of selective forgiveness. This is the lie that suggests others are deserving of God's forgiveness, but we have done things God could never forgive. As Christians, we understand that we're all on the outside looking in when it comes to God's holiness and our sinfulness. It is in this place outside that we would have remained unless God opened the door for our return. However, many people have bought into the deception that others are somehow deserving of God's forgiveness, but they are not. It's a lie from the pit of hell, and it smells like smoke! All Satan has to do to make it work is get us to agree. I fear that those in the church have often become unwitting pawns in his ongoing game of deception, for in our focus on "doing" rather than on "being," we have turned the gospel of grace into a spiritual merit badge system. Within *that* frame of reference, no one measures up.

As the country song suggests, the world today is looking for love in all the wrong places.[86] And they'll keep looking in the wrong places unless someone directs them to the right place. As the bride of Christ, the church (the body of Jesus in the world) has the most compelling, most relevant, most hopeful message the world has ever heard. We just have to make certain we proclaim it accurately.

In the course of our short journey together, we have considered the release, the redemption, and the recapitulation inherent to the atoning work of Jesus Christ—God in human flesh. By virtue of this comprehensive work, we have been purchased from the evil one, released from sin's bondage, cleansed of sin's defilement, reconciled to a loving God, and empowered for holy living. As Christ's ambassadors in a lost and dying world, we now have the privilege of living among those similarly afflicted and helping them to experience the same wholeness in Christ that we have been so privileged to receive. One day God will call all his ambassadors home, and we will celebrate the marvelous way God's precious human creation was rescued from the brink of disaster.

The prophet Jeremiah records God's prophetic message to his people living in Palestine whose sin would see them exiled into Babylonian captivity. Even as their unfaithfulness leads them into pain, misery, and heartache, his message is one of encouragement and comfort: "'For I know the plans I have for you,' declares the Lord, 'plans to prosper you and not to harm you, plans to give you hope and a future'" (Jeremiah 29:11). Even though they would experience the consequences of life lived wrongly, God promised them his sustaining presence to guide them through the worst of it.

He also promised them that there would come a time when they would be reunited with him in loving relationship.

In the same way, God announces his ongoing plan for those held in sin's captivity through the church. It is a plan of prosperity, not of punishment; it is a plan of hope, not of harm. This is God's message to the world, and it must be ours as well.

The atonement is the consummate work of God in restoring us to life-giving fellowship with him. And it is a message our world is literally dying to hear. We dare not deliver anything less. "For God so loved the world that he gave his one and only Son, that whoever believes in him shall not perish but have eternal life. For God did not send his Son into the world to condemn the world, but to save the world through him" (John 3:16–17). Hallelujah!

Relevance

REFLECTION QUESTIONS

1. How would you respond to the question my friend raised at our Bible study?

2. How would you defend the gospel's relevance to a skeptical friend?

3. We asserted that the church today is largely viewed as irrelevant. Do you agree? If so, why is it considered irrelevant? If you don't agree, give examples of how the world affirms the relevance of the church.

4. We suggested that it is a waste of time telling sinners they are sinners. Do you agree? Why or why not?

5. Do you believe God has forgiven you? Have you forgiven yourself?

6. We suggested that God's plan for the world is one of hope, love, and intimacy. Do you agree? Why or why not?

7. Have you accepted God's offer of intimacy in Christ?

Scriptures Cited

Introduction
1 Thessalonians 4:17

Chapter 1: Rudiments

John 1:1–3
Ecclesiastes 1:9
2 Corinthians 5:19
Romans 13:9
John 1:29

Mark 10:45
1 Corinthians 15:55
Colossians 3:14
2 Peter 3:8
Revelation 13:8

Chapter 2: Reorientation

John 3:17
2 Corinthians 6:14
Ephesians 2:13–16
Luke 6:45
Romans 5:8
Ephesians 2:8
Deuteronomy 30:19

Numbers 14:19
Matthew 18:22
Colossians 3:13
1 John 1:9
Matthew 6:14–15
2 Corinthians 5:19
2 Peter 2:9

Psalm 103:11–12
Ephesians 2:1–3

Romans 1:18
Romans 6:23

Chapter 3: Redemption

1 Peter 1:11–12
1 Corinthians 6:19–20
Acts 20:28
1 Corinthians 7:23
Revelation 5:9

Genesis 3:5
John 15:15
2 Corinthians 5:19
1 Peter 2:9b
1 Peter 2:9a

Chapter 4: Recapitulation

2 Corinthians 1:22
2 Corinthians 5:21
John 1:1
John 1:14
John 1:29
John 1:1, 14
John 1:29
Rom 3:25
Luke 15:22
Proverbs 26:11
2 Peter 2:20–22

Hebrews 6:4–6
1 Corinthians 10:13
John 14:12–14
Galatians 2:20
Leviticus 11:44
1 Peter 1:15–16
Matthew 5:48
Ephesians 3:20
2 Corinthians 5:17
1 John 4:4
Psalm 56:11

Chapter 5: Resolution

1 Peter 3:15
Ephesians 3:18
Hebrews 4:15
Romans 5:12
Ezekiel 18:20
John 3:6
Colossians 1:15
Romans 8:29
1 Corinthians 15:49

2 Corinthians 3:18
Philippians 3:21
1 John 3:2
Ephesians 6:12
Genesis 3:6
1 John 2:15–17
Luke 4:3
Luke 4:5–7
Luke 4:9

Scriptures Cited

Hebrews 12:1
Psalm 51:4
2 Samuel 11:18–24
2 Samuel 12:13
Romans 8:38–39
Proverbs 18:10
2 Corinthians 5:1
Luke 6:38
Romans 12:1–2
John 10:29

1 John 4:4
James 2:26
Romans 7:24
John 17:20–21
1 John 4:16–19
Genesis 1:31
2 Corinthians 1:19–20
Zephaniah 3:17
1 John 4:8–9

Chapter 6: Relevance

John 6:53–56
John 6:67–68
Acts 2:42
Genesis 14:18–20
Hebrews 7:27

Romans 1:21–22
Romans 5:12
Romans 1:18
Jeremiah 29:11
John 3:16–17

Works Cited

Anselm. *Why God Became Man*. Translated by Colleran, Joseph M. Albany: Magi Books, Inc, 1969.

Asadourian, His Eminence Avak. "Punishment in Orthodox Atonement Thought," ed. Miller, Mark C. Al Hashemi, 2008.

"atonement." In *Merriam-Webster Online Dictionary*. Springfield: Merriam-Webster Inc, 2008.

Aulen, Gustav. *Christus Victor*. Translated by A. G. Hebert, M.A. 5 ed. London: Society for Promoting Christian Knowledge, 1931.

Bailey, Kenneth E. *Poets and Peasant and Through Peasant Eyes—A Literary-Cultural Approach to the Parables in Luke*. Grand Rapids: Wm. B. Eerdmans Publishing Co., 1976.

Berkhof, Lewis. *Systematic Theology*. Grand Rapids: Wm. B. Eerdmans Publishing Company, 1941.

Buschel, F. "Lytrosis." In *Theological Dictionary of the New Testament*, ed. Friedrich, Gerhard Kittel and Gerhard. Grand Rapids: William. B. Eerdmans Publishing Co., 1985.

Butler, Trent C., ed. *Holman Bible Dictionary*. Nashville: Holman Bible Publishers, 1991.

Calvin, John. "Institutes of the Christian Religion," ed. Whitehead, Doug. London: Bonham Norton, 1599.

Chalke, Steve, and Alan Mann. *The Lost Message of Jesus*. Grand Rapids: Zondervan, 2004.

"conciliate." In *Merriam-Webster Online Dictionary*. Springfield: Merriam-Webster, Inc., 2009.

Coniaris, Anthony M. *Introducing the Orthodox Church*. Minneapolis: Light and Life Publishing.

Crosby, Fanny J., and William J. Kirkpatrick. "Redeemed." In *Worship in Song*. Kansas City: Lillenas Publishing Co., 1972.

Cross, George. "The Theology of Schleiermacher—A Condensed Presentation of His Chief Work, "The Christian Faith." The University of Chicago Press, 1911.

Dunning, H. Ray. *Grace, Faith, and Holiness*. 1 ed. Kansas City: Beacon Hill Press of Kansas City, 1988.

Edwards, David, and John R. W. Stott. *Evangelical Essentials, a Liberal-Evangelical Dialogue*. Downers Grove: InterVarsity Press, 1988.

Edwards, Jonathan. "Sinners in the Hands of an Angry God." In *Selected Sermons by Jonathan Edwards*. Grand Rapids: Christian Classics Ethereal Library, 1741.

Elwell, Walter A., ed. *Evangelical Dictionary of Theology*. Grand Rapids: Baker Book House, 1984.

Featherstone, William R. "My Jesus, I Love Thee." In *Hymns for the Living Church*. Carol Stream: Hope Publishing Company, 1974.

Foote, Billy. "You Are My King" praise chorus. Brentwood: EMI Christian Music Publishing, 1996.

Francis, James Allan. "One Solitary Life." In *The Real Jesus and Other Sermons*, ed. Francis, James Allan. Philadelphia: Judson Press, 1926.

Works Cited

Green, Joel B., and Mark D. Baker. *Recovering the Scandal of the Cross*. Downers Grove: InterVarsity Press, 2000.

Grider, J. Kenneth. *A Wesleyan-Holiness Theology*. Kansas City: Beacon Hill Press, 1994.

Herrmann, H. "The Theological Dictionary of the New Testament (Electronic Edition—Logos Research Systems, Inc.)." In *Katallasso*, ed. Kittell, G., G Friedrich and G.W. Bromiley, III: Wm. B. Eerdmans, 1985.

Hillar, Marian. "Laelius and Faustus Socini: Founders of Socinianism—Their Lives and Theology." *The Journal From the Radical Reformation* 10, no. 2 and 3, (2002).

Hilton, Ronald. *Demcracy and Churchill* Stanford: Stanford University, 2003, accessed January 31, 2009; available from http://wais.stanford.edu/Democracy.

Hodge, Charles. *Systematic Theology—Volume 2*. Vol. 2. 3 vols. Grand Rapids: William B. Eerdmans Co., 1941.

Irenaeus. "Against Heresies." In *Ante-Nicene Fathers*, ed. Roberts, Alexander, James Donaldson and A. Cleveland Coxe, I. Buffalo: Christian Literature Publishing.

Kent, William. *Doctrine of the Atonement* [web page]. New York: Robert Appleton Company, 2008, accessed December 9, 2008; available from. http://www.newadvent.org/cathen/02055a.htm

Ladd, G. Eldon. *A Theology of the New Testament*. Grand Rapids: Wm. B. Eerdmans Publishing Co., 1974.

Lee, Johnny. "Lookin' for Love." Lyrics. Atlanta: Q Records, 1989.

McKnight, Scott. *A Community Called Atonement* (Living Theology), ed. Jones, Tony. Nashville: Abingdon Press, 2007.

Neuhaus, Richard John. *Death on a Friday Afternoon*. New York: Basic, 2000.

Pavel, Fr. Mihai. "Punishment in Orthodox Atonement Thought," ed. Miller, Mark C. Al Hashemia, 2008.

Peretti, Frank. *Piercing the Darkness*. Westchester: Crossway Books, 1989.

Rashdall, Hastings. "Philosophy and Religion—Six Lectures Delivered at Cambridge," ed. Haines, Al: Duckworth and Co., 2007.

Renn, Stephen D., ed. *Expository Dictionary of Bible Words*. Peabody: Hendrickson Publishers, Inc, 2005.

Robinson, B. A. *The Penal Theory a.k.a. The Penal Substitution Theory* Ontario: Ontario Consultants on Religous Tolerance, April 13, 2005, accessed February 24, 2009; available from www.religoustolerance.org/chr_atone10.htm.

Sayers, Dorothy L. *The Mind of the Maker*. San Francisco: HarperSanFrancisco, 1941.

Scofield, C. I., Henry G. Weston, and James M. Gray, eds. *The Old Scofield Study Bible*. Oxford: Oxford University Press, 1917.

Stamoolis, James J., ed. *Three Views on Eastern Orthodoxy and Evangelicalism*. Edited by Gundry, Stanley N., Counterpoints—Exploring Theology. Grand Rapids: Zondervan, 2004.

Stăniloae, Dumitru. *The Experience of God*. London: Continuum International Publishing Group, 1994.

Statistics, Bureau of Justice. *Recidivism* Washington, D.C.: U. S. Department of Justice, 2007, accessed February 14, 2009 http://www.ojp.usdoj.gov/bjs/crimoff.htm#recidivism.

Strobel, Lee. *God's Outrageous Claims*. Vol. 1998. Grand Rapids: Zondervan, 1998.

Tillich, Paul. *The Eternal Now*. New York: Charles Scribner's Sons, 1963.

Victor, Paul Jacques Raymond Bins de Saint, and James J. O'Donnell, eds. *Confessions of St. Augustine, Bishop of Hippo*. London: Clark's, 1876.

Wall, Dr. Robert. "The Atonement." Seattle: Seattle Pacific University, 2008.

Works Cited

Wangerin, Walter. *The Ragman and Other Cries of Faith.* New York: HarperCollins, 1984.

Ware, Kallistos. *The Orthodox Way.* Crestwood: St. Vladimir's Seminary Press, 1979.

Ware, Timothy. *The Orthodox Church.* London: Penguin Books, 1997.

Webster, Noah. "atone." In *Noah Webster's 1828 Dictionary (electronic version).* Franklin: Packard Technologies, 2003.

Wesley, Charles. "And Can It Be?" In *Worship in Song.* Kansas City: Lillenas Publishing Co., 1739.

———. "O For a Thousand Tongues." In *The Hymnal for Worship and Celebration*, ed. Fettke, Tom. Waco: Word Music, 1986.

Wesley, John. "The Sermons of John Wesley—Sermon 19." In *The Great Privilege of Those That Are Born of God*, ed. Jackson, Thomas: The Wesley Center for Applied Theology, 1872.

Wiley, H.. Orton. *Christian Theology.* Vol. 2. 3 vols. Kansas City: Beacon Hill Press, 1952.

Willard, Dallas. *The Divine Conspiracy.* San Francisco: HarperSanFrancisco, 1998.

Wright, N. T. *The Cross and the Cariatures* Wolverhampton: Fulcrum, 2007, accessed December 22, 2008; available from www.fulcrum-anglican.org.uk/page.cfm?ID=205.

Bibliography

Recidivism Washington, D.C.: U. S. Department of Justice, 2007, accessed February 14, 2009, http://www.ojp.usdoj.gov/bjs/crimoff.htm#recidivism.

"atonement." In *Merriam-Webster Online Dictionary*. Springfield: Merriam-Webster Inc, 2008.

"conciliate." In *Merriam-Webster Online Dictionary*. Springfield: Merriam-Webster, Inc., 2009.

"repent." In *Merriam-Webster Online Dictionary*. Springfield: Merriam-Webster, Inc., 2009.

(staff). "Quotes for the White Witch from the Chronicles of Narnia." IMDb.com, 2005.

(staff). "Why Did Jesus Die?" In *BBC—Religion and Ethics*, 2005. www.bbc.co.uk/religion/religions/christianity/beliefs/whydidjesusdie_1.shtml

(staff). *Qualitative* Research San Francisco: Wikimedia Foundation, 2008, accessed April 14, 2008; available from http://en.wikipedia.org/wiki/Qualitative_research.

———. *Quantitative Research* San Francisco: Wikimedia Foundation, 2008, accessed April 14, 2008; available from http://en.wikipedia.org/wiki/Quantitative_research.

Anselm. *Why God Became Man*. Translated by Colleran, Joseph M. Albany: Magi Books, Inc, 1969.

Asadourian, His Eminence Avak. "Punishment in Orthodox Atonement Thought," ed. Miller, Mark C. Al Hashemi, 2008.

Athanasius. "Incarnation of the Word." In *Nicene and Post-Nicene Fathers, Second Series*, ed. Schaff, Philip, 4. Buffalo: Christian Literature Publishing.

Augustine. "Exposition on Psalm 126." In *Nicene and Post-Nicene Fathers*, ed. Schaff, Philip, 8. Buffalo: Christian Literature Publishing Company, ~400.

———. "The City of God." In *Nicene and Post-Nicene Fathers*, ed. Schaff, Philip, 2. New York: Christian Literature Publishing Company, 410.

Aulen, Gustav. *Christus Victor*. Translated by A. G. Hebert, M.A. 5 ed. London: Society for Promoting Christian Knowledge, 1931.

Bailey, Kenneth E. *Poets and Peasant and Through Peasant Eyes—A Literary-Cultural Approach to the Parables in Luke*. Grand Rapids: Wm. B. Eerdmans Publishing Co., 1976.

Bakke, Ray, and Jon Sharpe. *Street Signs: A New Direction in Urban Ministry*. Birmingham: New Hope Publishers, 2006.

Barker, Kenneth, ed. *The Holy Bible, New International Version*. Grand Rapids: Zondervan, 1984.

Berkhof, Lewis. *Systematic Theology*. Grand Rapids: Wm. B. Eerdmans Publishing Company, 1941.

Boersma, Hans. "Eschatological Justice and the Cross." *Theology Today* 60, no. 2 (2003): 1.

_____. "Penal Substitution and the Possibility of Unconditional Hospitality." *Scottish Journal of Theology* 57, no. 1 (2004): 1.

Boudreaux, Jonathan. *Baretta* tvdvdreviews.com 2003, accessed February 24, 2008; available from www.tvdvdreviews.com.

Bray, Gerald. *Romans*. Vol. VI Ancient Christian Commentary on Scripture, ed. Oden, Thomas C. Downer's Grove: InterVarsity Press, 1998.

_____. *Romans*. Vol. VI Ancient Christian Commentary on Scripture, ed. Oden, Thomas. Downer's Grove: InterVarsity, 1998.

Burke, Robert M. "Appreciative Inquiry: A Literature Review." In *LTU CIMBA*. Southfield: Lawrence Technological University, 2001.

Buschel, F. "Lytrosis." In *Theological Dictionary of the New Testament*, ed. Friedrich, Gerhard Kittel and Gerhard. Grand Rapids: William. B. Eerdmans Publishing Co., 1985.

Butler, Trent C., ed. *Holman Bible Dictionary*. Nashville: Holman Bible Publishers, 1991.

Calvin, John. "Institutes of the Christian Religion," ed. Whitehead, Doug. London: Bonham Norton, 1599.

Carr, Amy. "Deceiving the Devil." *The Journal of Religion* 81, no. 2 (2001).

Chalke, Steve. "Cross Purposes." In *Christianity*, 2004.

Chalke, Steve, and Alan Mann. *The Lost Message of Jesus*. Grand Rapids: Zondervan, 2004.

Chrysostom, John. *The Paschal Sermon of St. John Chrysostomos* Perth: Ecumenical Patriarchate of Australia, May 4, 2008 400, accessed June 5 2008; available from www.orthodoxchristian.info.

Ciobotea, Daniel. *Confessing the Truth in Love*. Bucharest: Trinitas, 2001.

Coniaris, Anthony M. *Introducing the Orthodox Church.* Minneapolis: Light and Life Publishing.

Crosby, Fanny J., and William J. Kirkpatrick. "Redeemed." In *Worship in Song.* Kansas City: Lillenas Publishing Co., 1972.

Cross, George. "The Theology of Schleiermacher—A Condensed Presentation of His Chief Work, "The Christian Faith." The University of Chicago Press, 1911.

Dever, Mark. "Nothing But the Blood." In *ChristianityToday.com*, 50, 6, 2006.

Dunning, H. Ray. *Grace, Faith, and Holiness.* 1 ed. Kansas City: Beacon Hill Press of Kansas City, 1988.

Edwards, David, and John R. W. Stott. *Evangelical Essentials, a Liberal-Evangelical Dialogue.* Downers Grove: InterVarsity Press, 1988.

Edwards, Jonathan. "Sinners in the Hands of an Angry God." Selected Sermons by Jonathan Edwards. Grand Rapids: Christian Classics Ethereal Library, 1741.

Elwell, Walter A., ed. *Evangelical Dictionary of Theology.* Grand Rapids: Baker Book House, 1984.

Evans, Gillian R. *Bernard of Clairvaux.* New York: Oxford University Press, 2000.

Featherstone, William R. "My Jesus, I Love Thee." In *Hymns for the Living Church.* Carol Stream: Hope Publishing Company, 1974.

Finlan, Stephen. *Problems With Atonement: The Origins of, and Controversy About, the Atonement Doctrine.* Collegeville: Liturgical Press, 2005.

Flood, Derek. "Understanding the Cross: Penal Substitution vs. Christus Victor." In *The Rebel God*, 2007, 2000.

Foote, Billy. "You Are My King." Praise chorus. Brentwood: EMI Christian Music Publishing, 1996.

Bibliography

Francis, James Allan. "One Solitary Life." In *The Real Jesus and Other Sermons*, ed. Francis, James Allan. Philadelphia: Judson Press, 1926.

Gonzalez, Justo L. *The Story of Christianity—Volume 1*. Vol. 1. 2 vols. San Francisco: HarperCollins, 1985.

_____. *The Story of Christianity—Volume 2*. Vol. 2. 2 vols. San Francisco: HarperCollins, 1985.

Greathouse, William M. "Sanctification and the Christus Victor Motif in Wesleyan Theology." In *Wesleyan Theological Journal*, 7, 1972.

Green, Joel B., and Mark D. Baker. *Recovering the Scandal of the Cross*. Downers Grove: InterVarsity Press, 2000.

Grider, J. Kenneth. *A Wesleyan-Holiness Theology*. Kansas City: Beacon Hill Press, 1994.

Griffin, Winn, and Brian McLaren. *God's EPIC Adventure*. Woodinville: Harmon Press, 2007.

Hastings, Adrian. *150-550 A World History of Christianity*, ed. Hastings, Adrian. Grand Rapids: William B. Eerdmans Publishing Co., 1999.

Hayes, Stephen. *Salvation and Atonement* Tshwane: Wordpress.com, 2008, accessed December 1, 2008; available from http://khanya.wordpress.com/2008/06/30/salvation-and-atonement.

Herman, Nicholas (Brother Lawrence). *The Practice of the Presence of God*. Grand Rapids: Spire, 1967.

Herrmann, H. "The Theological Dictionary of the New Testament (Electronic Edition—Logos Research Systems, Inc.)." In *Katallasso*, ed. Kittell, G., G Friedrich and G.W. Bromiley, III: Wm. B. Eerdmans, 1985.

Hillar, Marian. "Laelius and Faustus Socini: Founders of Socinianism—Their Lives and Theology." *The Journal From the Radical Reformation* 10, no. 2 & 3 (2002).

Hilton, Ronald. *Democracy and Churchill* Stanford: Stanford University, 2003, accessed January 31, 2009; available from http://wais.stanford.edu/Democracy.

Hodge, Charles. *Systematic Theology—Volume 2*. Vol. 2. 3 vols. Grand Rapids: William B. Eerdmans Co., 1941.

Holmes, Steve. "Can Punishment Bring Peace?" *Scottish Journal of Theology* 58, no. 1 (2005): 1.

Irenaeus. "Against Heresies." In *Ante-Nicene Fathers*, ed. Roberts, Alexander, James Donaldson and A. Cleveland Coxe, I. Buffalo: Christian Literature Publishing.

Keck, Eric. *Atonement* [Electronic]. 2008, accessed April 7, 2008; available from www.pneumanaut.com/journal.

Kent, William. *Doctrine of the Atonement* [web page]. New York: Robert Appleton Company, 2008, accessed December 9, 2008; available from www.newadvent.org/cathen/02055a.htm

Kim, Seyoon. "The Atoning Death of Christ on the Cross." In *Theology News and Notes*, 55, 4, 2008.

Ladd, G. Eldon. *A Theology of the New Testament*. Grand Rapids: Wm. B. Eerdmans Publishing Co., 1974.

Lee, Johnny. "Lookin' for Love." Lyrics. Atlanta: Q Records, 1989.

Lewis, C. S. *The Lion, the Witch, and the Wardrobe*. New York: McMillan Publishing Co., 1950.

———. *Mere Christianity*. New York: Touchstone, 1952.

———. *The Lion, the Witch, and the Wardrobe*. New York: HarperCollins, 1978.

Lightner, Jean K. "Identification of species within the sheep-goat kind (Tsoan monobaramin)," in *Journal of Creation* 20(3), 2006

Luther, Martin. *Shorter Catechism* Ft. Wayne: Concordia Theological Seminary, 2006, accessed June 21, 2008; available from www.projectwittenberg.org.

Bibliography

McKnight, Scott. *A Community Called Atonement* (Living Theology), ed. Jones, Tony. Nashville: Abingdon Press, 2007.

Moore, Jessica. "Come Learn From Three Sages." Seattle: Bakke Graduate University, 2008.

Myers, William R. *Research in Ministry, a Primer for the Doctor of Ministry Program*. Chicago: Exploration Press, 2000.

Neuhaus, Richard John. *Death on a Friday Afternoon*. New York: Basic, 2000.

Pavel, Fr. Mihai. "Punishment in Orthodox Atonement Thought," ed. Miller, Mark C. Al Hashemia, 2008.

Peretti, Frank. *Piercing the Darkness*. Westchester: Crossway Books, 1989.

Quay, Stephanie. *Baretta: The Stone Conspiracy* [television]. CNET Networks Entertainment, 1978, accessed April 10, 2008; available from www.tv.com/baretta.

Rashdall, Hastings. "Philosophy and Religion—Six Lectures Delivered at Cambridge," ed. Haines, Al: Duckworth and Co., 2007.

Renn, Stephen D., ed. *Expository Dictionary of Bible Words*. Peabody: Hendrickson Publishers, Inc, 2005.

Robinson, B. A. *The Penal Theory a.k.a. The Penal Substitution Theory* Ontario: Ontario Consultants on Religious Tolerance, April 13, 2005 2004, accessed February 24, 2009; available from www.religoustolerance.org/chr_atone10.htm.

Robinson, Jeff. "Study: Recent Grads 3 times more likely to be Calvinists." In *Baptist Press*, 2007.

Sayers, Dorothy L. *The Mind of the Maker*. San Francisco: HarperSanFrancisco, 1941.

Schlumpf, Heidi. "For Us and for Our Salvation." *U. S. Catholic* 70, no. 3 (2005): 6.

Scofield, C. I., Henry G. Weston, and James M. Gray, eds. *The Old Scofield Study Bible*. Oxford: Oxford University Press, 1917.

Self, William L. "Faith." In *The Holman Bible Dictionary*, ed. Butler, Trent C. Nashville: Holman Bible Publishers, 1991.

———. "Faith." In *Holman Bible Dictionary*, ed. Butler, Trent C. Nashville: Holman Bible Publishers, 1991.

Shamoun, Sam. *Islam's Doctrine of Substitutionary Atonement and the Ransoming of Sinners* Charlottesville: 2002, accessed February 4, 2008; available from www.answering-islam.org.

Shelton, R. Larry. *Cross & Covenant*. Tyrone: Paternoster, 2006.

Staff. *McDonald's Scalding Coffee Case* Washington, D.C.: American Association for Justice, 2008, accessed February 24, 2008; available from www.atla.org/PressRoom/FACTS/frivolous/McdonaldsCoffeecase.aspx.

Stamoolis, James J., ed. *Three Views on Eastern Orthodoxy and Evangelicalism*. Edited by Gundry, Stanley N., Counterpoints—Exploring Theology. Grand Rapids: Zondervan, 2004.

Stăniloae, Dumitru. *The Experience of God*. London: Continuum International Publishing Group, 1994.

Steele, Dr. Richard. "The Atonement." Seattle: Seattle Pacific University, 2008.

Strobel, Lee. *God's Outrageous Claims*. Vol. 1998. Grand Rapids: Zondervan, 1998.

Tillich, Paul. *The Eternal Now*. New York: Charles Scribner's Sons, 1963.

Victor, Paul Jacques Raymond Bins de Saint, and James J. O'Donnell, eds. *Confessions of St. Augustine, Bishop of Hippo*. London: Clark's, 1876.

Bibliography

Vincent, John Martin. *Huldreich Zwingli* Heroes of the Reformation: A Series of Biographies of the Leaders of the Protestant Reformation, ed. Jackson, Samuel Macauley. New York: G. P. Putnam's Sons, 1903.

Volf, Miroslav. *Free of Charge: Giving and Forgiving in a Culture Stripped of Grace.* Grand Rapids: Zondervan, 2005.

Wall, Dr. Robert. "The Atonement." Seattle: Seattle Pacific University, 2008.

Wangerin, Walter. *The Ragman and Other Cries of Faith.* New York: HarperCollins, 1984.

Ware, Kallistos. *The Orthodox Way.* Crestwood: St. Vladimir's Seminary Press, 1979.

Ware, Timothy. *The Orthodox Church.* London: Penguin Books, 1997.

Weaver, J. Denny. *The Non-Violent Atonement.* Grand Rapids: Wm. B. Eerdmans, 2001.

Webster, Noah. "atone." In *Noah Webster's 1828 Dictionary (electronic version).* Franklin: Packard Technologies, 2003.

Wesley, Charles. "And Can It Be?" In *Worship in Song.* Kansas City: Lillenas Publishing Co., 1739.

_____. "O For a Thousand Tongues." In *The Hymnal for Worship and Celebration,* ed. Fettke, Tom. Waco: Word Music, 1986.

Wesley, John. "The Sermons of John Wesley—Sermon 19." In *The Great Privilege of Those That Are Born of God,* ed. Jackson, Thomas: The Wesley Center for Applied Theology, 1872.

Wilder, William N. *The Doctrine of Justification in the Work of N. T. Wright* Charlottesville: The Center for Christian Study, 2005, accessed February 4, 2008; available from www.studycenter.net/NTWright-Justification.htm.

Wiley, H. Orton. *Christian Theology.* Vol. 2. 3 vols. Kansas City: Beacon Hill Press, 1952.

Willard, Dallas. *The Divine Conspiracy*. San Francisco: HarperSanFrancisco, 1998.

Williams, Stuart Murray. "Stuart Murray Williams on the Lost Message of Jesus." In *Anabaptist Network*, 2004.

Wright, N. T. "Q&A." In *Wrightsaid*. Durham, 2005.

_____. *The Cross and the Caricatures* Wolverhampton: Fulcrum, 2007, accessed December 22, 2008; available from www.fulcrum-anglican.org.uk/page.cfm?ID=205.

_____. *Surprised By Hope*. New York: HarperCollins, 2008.

Wynkoop, Mildred Bangs. *A Theology of Love*. Kansas City: Beacon Hill Press of Kansas City, 1972.

Young, Pamela Dickey. "Beyond Moral Influence to an Atoning Life." *Theology Today* 52, no. 3 (1995): 12.

Endnotes

Introduction
1. check out www.seattleparagliding.com

Chapter 1: Rudiments
2. Peretti, Frank, *Piercing the Darkness* (Westchester: Crossway Books, 1989), 441.
3. Wesley, Charles, "And Can It Be?," in *Worship in Song* (Kansas City: Lillenas Publishing Co., 1739).
4. Renn, Stephen D., ed., *Expository Dictionary of Bible Words* (Peabody: Hendrickson Publishers, Inc, 2005), 221-222.
5. Kent, William, *Doctrine of the Atonement* [web page] (Robert Appleton Company, 2008, accessed December 9 2008).
6. Scofield, C. I., Henry G. Weston, and James M. Gray, eds., *The Old Scofield Study Bible* (Oxford: Oxford University Press, 1917), 148.
7. Neuhaus, Richard John, *Death on a Friday Afternoon* (New York: Basic, 2000), 15.

8. Ladd, G. Eldon, *A Theology of the New Testament* (Grand Rapids: Wm. B. Eerdmans Publishing Co., 1974), 464.
9. Butler, Trent C., ed., *Holman Bible Dictionary* (Nashville: Holman Bible Publishers, 1991), 128-129.
10. Elwell, Walter A., ed., *Evangelical Dictionary of Theology* (Grand Rapids: Baker Book House, 1984), 97.
11. Renn, ed., 163.
12. Webster, Noah, "atone," in *Noah Webster's 1828 Dictionary (electronic version)* (Franklin: Packard Technologies, 2003).
13. "atonement," in *Merriam-Webster Online Dictionary* (Springfield: Merriam-Webster Inc, 2008).
14. Berkhof, Lewis, *Systematic Theology* (Grand Rapids: Wm. B. Eerdmans Publishing Company, 1941), 367.
15. Ibid., 373.
16. Grider, J. Kenneth, *A Wesleyan-Holiness Theology* (Kansas City: Beacon Hill Press, 1994), 322.
17. Green, Joel B. and Mark D. Baker, *Recovering the Scandal of the Cross* (Downers Grove: InterVarsity Press, 2000), 119-123.
18. Aulen, Gustav, *Christus Victor*, trans. A. G. Hebert, M.A., 5 ed. (London: Society for Promoting Christian Knowledge, 1931), 21.
19. Green and Baker, 119.
20. Wangerin, Walter, *The Ragman and Other Cries of Faith* (New York: HarperCollins, 1984).
21. Lightner, Jean K., "Identification of species within the sheep-goat kind (Tsoan monobaramin)," in *Journal of Creation* (Eight Mile Plains, 2006), 61-65
22. Aulen, 58.
23. Irenaeus, "Against Heresies," in *Ante-Nicene Fathers*, ed. Roberts, Alexander, James Donaldson, and A. Cleveland Coxe (Buffalo: Christian Literature Publishing), 3.19.1.

24. Aulen, 66-67.
25. Green and Baker, 123.
26. Ibid.
27. Ibid., 127.
28. Ibid., 21.
29. Anselm, *Why God Became Man*, trans. Colleran, Joseph M. (Albany: Magi Books, Inc, 1969), 72-73.
30. Green and Baker, 22.
31. Aulen, 109.
32. Calvin, John, "Institutes of the Christian Religion," ed. Whitehead, Doug (London: Bonham Norton, 1599), 2.15.6.
33. Hodge, Charles, *Systematic Theology—Volume 2*, 3 vols., vol. 2 (Grand Rapids: William B. Eerdmans Co., 1941), 361.
34. Ibid., 358-359.
35. Ibid., 362.
36. Edwards, David and John R. W. Stott, *Evangelical Essentials, a Liberal-Evangelical Dialogue* (Downers Grove: InterVarsity Press, 1988), 109.
37. Hillar, Marian, "Laelius and Faustus Socini: Founders of Socinianism—Their Lives and Theology," *The Journal From the Radical Reformation* 10, no. 2 & 3 (2002).
38. Cross, George, "The Theology of Schleiermacher—A Condensed Presentation of His Chief Work, "The Christian Faith" (The University of Chicago Press, 1911), 94-95.
39. Rashdall, Hastings, "Philosophy and Religion—Six Lectures Delivered at Cambridge," ed. Haines, Al (Duckworth and Co., 2007), 153-156.
40. Tillich, Paul, *The Eternal Now* (New York: Charles Scribner's Sons, 1963).

Chapter 2: Reorientation

41. Herrmann, H., "The Theological Dictionary of the New Testament (Electronic Edition—Logos Research Systems, Inc.)," in *Katallasso*, ed. Kittell, G., G Friedrich, and G.W. Bromiley (Wm. B. Eerdmans, 1985).
42. "conciliate," in *Merriam-Webster Online Dictionary* (Springfield: Merriam-Webster, Inc., 2009).
43. Featherstone, William R., "My Jesus, I Love Thee," in *Hymns for the Living Church* (Carol Stream: Hope Publishing Company, 1974).
44. Foote, Billy, *You Are My King*, 1996, EMI Christian Music Publishing, Brentwood.
45. Robinson, B. A., *The Penal Theory a.k.a. The Penal Substitution Theory* (Ontario Consultants on Religous Tolerance, April 13, 2005 2004, accessed February 24 2009); available from www.religoustolerance.org/chr_atone10.htm.
46. Coniaris, Anthony M., *Introducing the Orthodox Church* (Minneapolis: Light and Life Publishing), 62.
47. Pavel, Fr. Mihai, "Punishment in Orthodox Atonement Thought," ed. Miller, Mark C. (Al Hashemia: 2008).
48. Stamoolis, James J., ed., *Three Views on Eastern Orthodoxy and Evangelicalism*, ed. Gundry, Stanley N., Counterpoints—Exploring Theology (Grand Rapids: Zondervan, 2004), 172.
49. Pavel.
50. Stăniloae, Dumitru, *The Experience of God* (London: Continuum International Publishing Group, 1994), 209.
51. Coniaris, 69.
52. Francis, James Allan, "One Solitary Life," in *The Real Jesus and Other Sermons*, ed. Francis, James Allan (Philadelphia: Judson Press, 1926).

53. Hilton, Ronald, *Demcracy and Churchill*(Stanford University, 2003, accessed January 31, 2009 2009); available from http://wais.stanford.edu/Democracy.
54. Edwards, Jonathan, "Sinners in the Hands of an Angry God," in *Selected Sermons by Jonathan Edwards* (Grand Rapids: Christian Classics Ethereal Library, 1741), 10.
55. Chalke, Steve and Alan Mann, *The Lost Message of Jesus* (Grand Rapids: Zondervan, 2004), 56.
56. Sayers, Dorothy L., *The Mind of the Maker* (San Francisco: Harper San Francisco, 1941), 12.
57. Ibid.
58. Wright, N. T., *The Cross and the Cariatures* (Fulcrum, 2007, accessed December 22, 2008); available from www.fulcrum-anglican.org.uk/page.cfm?ID=205.
59. Chalke and Mann, 66-67.

Chapter 3: Redemption
60. Buschel, F., "Lytrosis," in *Theological Dictionary of the New Testament*, ed. Friedrich, Gerhard Kittel and Gerhard (Grand Rapids: William. B. Eerdmans Publishing Co., 1985), Volume IV, 335-356.
61. Crosby, Fanny J. and William J. Kirkpatrick, "Redeemed," in *Worship in Song* (Kansas City: Lillenas Publishing Co., 1972).
62. Strobel, Lee, *God's Outrageous Claims*, vol. 1998 (Grand Rapids: Zondervan, 1998), 194.
63. Aulen, 67.
64. Wesley, Charles, "O For a Thousand Tongues," in *The Hymnal for Worship and Celebration*, ed. Fettke, Tom (Waco: Word Music, 1986).
65. Lewis, C.S., *The Lion, the Witch, and the Wardrobe* (New York: McMillan Publishing Co., 1950), 152.

Chapter 4: Recapitulation
66. Ibid. 160.
67. Renn, ed., 766.
68. Ware, Timothy, *The Orthodox Church* (London: Penguin Books, 1997), 229.
69. Asadourian, His Eminence Avak, "Punishment in Orthodox Atonement Thought," ed. Miller, Mark C. (Al Hashemi: 2008).
70. Bailey, Kenneth E., *Poets and Peasant and Through Peasant Eyes—A Literary-Cultural Approach to the Parables in Luke* (Grand Rapids: Wm. B. Eerdmans Publishing Co., 1976).
71. Statistics, Bureau of Justice, *Recidivism* (U. S. Department of Justice, 2007, accessed February 14, 2009); available from http://www.ojp.usdoj.gov/bjs/crimoff.htm#recidivism.
72. Wesley, John, "The Sermons of John Wesley—Sermon 19," in *The Great Privilege of Those That Are Born of God*, ed. Jackson, Thomas (The Wesley Center for Applied Theology, 1872).
73. Willard, Dallas, *The Divine Conspiracy* (San Francisco: HarperSanFrancisco, 1998), 35.
74. Ibid., 36-37.
75. Ibid., 58.

Chapter 5: Resolution
76. McKnight, Scott, *A Community Called Atonement*, ed. Jones, Tony, (Living Theology) (Nashville: Abingdon Press, 2007), 23.
77. Dunning, H. Ray, *Grace, Faith, and Holiness*, 1 ed. (Kansas City: Beacon Hill Press of Kansas City, 1988), 301.
78. Wiley, H.. Orton, *Christian Theology*, 3 vols., vol. 2 (Kansas City: Beacon Hill Press, 1952), 98.

79. Ware, Kallistos, *The Orthodox Way* (Crestwood: St. Vladimir's Seminary Press, 1979), 62.
80. Ibid., 60.
81. McKnight, 24.
82. Butler, ed., 469.
83. Wall, Dr. Robert, "The Atonement," (Seattle: Seattle Pacific University, 2008).
84. Ware, *The Orthodox Way*, 62.

Chapter 6: Relevance
85. Victor, Paul Jacques Raymond Bins de Saint and James J. O'Donnell, eds., *Confessions of St. Augustine, Bishop of Hippo* (London: Clark's, 1876), Book 1, Page 1.
86. Lee, Johnny, *Lookin' for Love*, Music, 1989, Q Records, Atlanta.

WinePressPublishing
Your Book, Defined.
Since 1991.

To order additional copies of this book call:
1-877-421-READ (7323)
or please visit our website at
www.WinePressbooks.com

If you enjoyed this quality custom-published book,
drop by our website for more books and information.

www.winepresspublishing.com
"Your partner in custom publishing."

LaVergne, TN USA
26 January 2011
214007LV00003B/71/P